My War Years in London

(Diary of an Actress)

Rona Laurie

ISBN 978-1-4452-8436-1

*Dedicated to the memory of
John Gielgud - a peerless actor.*

BY THE SAME AUTHOR

The Actor's Art and Craft
A Hundred Speeches From the Theatre
Scenes and Ideas
Festivals and Adjudication
Auditioning
Children's Plays from Beatrix Potter

ACKNOWLEDGEMENTS

I would like to thank Mark Schottlander for his help and advice, and Phillipa Neilson and Jo Jo Kelly for their patient support.

CONTENTS

❧ PROLOGUE ❧
1916 - 1934

As I approached my ninetieth birthday, I came under increasing pressure from friends and students to write an account of my war-time experiences, first as a student at the Royal Academy of Dramatic Art and then as a young actress in repertory, on tour and finally in the West End during London's blitz in World War Two.

I had kept day to day diaries for the years 1938 - 1944, as well as the programmes of the plays that I had seen, with criticisms, sometimes pungent of the director and cast scribbled in them. I also had a collection of professional and family photographs taken at all stages of my life. And so I agreed to embark on this somewhat daunting task.

As I began to look back, I realised that I ought to explain how I came to enter the profession, which I have never left, by describing my background, early childhood, schooldays and years at the university.

Throughout I use the word "actress" instead of following the "in" habit of referring to both sexes as "actors", a fashion which I regard as an affectation and which often leads to ambiguity. The diaries are more to do with the theatre and my social life than with the war. I make passing reference to the price of a drink, of a packet of cigarettes, of meals in restaurants and café's.

The requirement of clothing coupons made a big impact on our lives. We would have killed to get enough to buy a pair of silk stockings.

I had a number of boyfriends, simultaneously rather than consecutively. This, of course, led to complications, for example on the occasion when, by mistake, I asked two rivals to join me during the same weekend when I was on tour. Most of these suitors were in the forces, or waiting to be called up and I had met them when I was an undergraduate at Birmingham University. I had several proposals of marriage. The reason for this, I am sure, was the pre-war atmosphere. Young men were anxious to get married before they were posted overseas, just as they had been before the First World War. And in those days the men far outnumbered the women in universities. This meant that I nearly always had four or five invitations to the dances and hops.

At this point I should explain that when I wrote in the diary 'He tried to make love to me' this didn't mean that he expected sexual intercourse, as it probably would today, but it implied no more than a chaste kiss on the cheek, or on the mouth, with closed lips of course, a cuddle or a warm embrace. In the thirties and forties the boy always paid the bill at restaurants, cafés, nightclubs and pubs and bought our tickets for theatres and cinemas. There was no such thing as 'going Dutch' except when two students went out together. I now realise that those dates never cost me a thing, which was a mercy. As regards presents, there was a strict etiquette; chocolates, flowers and gloves were allowed, but nothing else, except of course clothing coupons which were always gratefully accepted.

In the thirties, young men were beginning to own cars. My mother thought that this was a threat to our virginity "Now every man has his own mobile room to seduce you in" she said. She thought that taxis constituted an even greater risk and advised us, when going on a date, to wear 'taxi-cheaters'. These were old-fashioned bloomers; knickers closed by elastic at the waist and knee and could be relied on to thwart any bold escort who attempted to take liberties when he was seeing us home after an evening out.

I often mention drinks and on reading the diaries I am amazed by the amount that I managed to put away, seldom having a hangover. This was remarkable, considering the awful mixtures that I swallowed. The warning 'never mix grape and grain', meant nothing to me then. I should add here that I have never had a drink problem in my life and my consumption of wine and spirits was considerably reduced after I left the theatre. There was one entry which mentioned cigarettes as costing a penny and a quarter each. This shocked me so much that I gave up smoking for seven weeks.

Another surprise was to realise how much energy we youngsters must have had, sometimes going to three or four night clubs in one evening and that after a demanding day's work at the Royal Academy of Dramatic Art. And then we had to be at a class at nine-thirty the next morning. Of course exhaustion sometimes caught up with us.

"What did it feel like to live in London during those years?" I am sometimes asked, and "Were you frightened during the blitz?" Strangely enough my dominant feeling was not so much one of fear but of terrible tiredness; the result of disturbed and sleepless nights spent in shelters, basements and cellars during air raids. I never slept in the underground, though many people did. One saw them huddled together on the platforms. Their cheerfulness and good humour was amazing.

I knew the extremes of sorrow and happiness. We led a heightened existence because the possibility of sudden, violent death was always with us as well as constant anxiety about the dangers to our friends, relations and fellow students. However my class-mates and I resolved to live life to the full while we had it, the 'Carpe Diem' philosophy. Now, looking back in 2008, the years 1938-1945 seem to merge into one long stretch of time, quite unlike anything that I'd known before, or was to know again. But, despite the horror and tragedy of war and the dangers of our day to day existence, it was an experience which I would not have missed for all the world.

ಔIಚಿ
1916 - 1934

CHILDHOOD AND SCHOOLDAYS.
How it all began

In 1938 the growing threat of war was hanging over the country. On the 26th September I wrote in my diary "War is terribly close, but I can't feel a thing." My father, who had served in the Royal Army Medical Corps in the First World War, was sent for by the war office and subsequently given the post of Assistant Director of Medical Services (ADMS) to an anti-aircraft division. We had gas masks fitted on that day. On the 30th the Prime Minister Neville Chamberlain came back from Germany, where he had gone to try to appease Hitler and appeared on the News clutching a three-page letter of congratulation from George VI 'written in His Majesty's own hand'. "I believe it is peace for our time, peace with honour" he assured the cheering crowds.

Earlier in that month I had been to London for an audition at the Royal Academy of Dramatic Art and had been accepted. This was not a sudden decision; a stage career had been my ambition from a very early age.

Now to describe my family background and upbringing and how I persisted with this aspiration throughout my school life from kindergarten, junior, secondary, public school and university. The title of this book is My War Years in London but on re-reading my diaries I have come to realise that they are more to do with the theatre than the war which featured as a background.

I was born in 1916 in Derby into a family with a medical background; my father, grandfather, two uncles and a cousin all being doctors. My father, a pioneer in radiology, was the consultant at the Derbyshire Royal Infirmary. He and my mother were enthusiastic amateurs and belonged to the Derby Shakespeare Society (founded in 1908) which gave annual performances at the Grand Theatre and now takes its production to the Minack Theatre in Cornwall every second year. My mother, whom we children always called "Mimi" played leading parts with them. Recently I was told about the occasion when she was playing Cleopatra. It was the death scene. When she was applying the venomous asp to her arm a Derbyshire voice called out from the gallery "'urry up luv, or the asp will die before you do". Alan Bates, as a schoolboy, was cast as Arthur in 'King John'. His talent was already evident, so it was no surprise when he entered the profession and had a distinguished career on stage, television and in films. He appeared in the original production of John Osborne's 'Look Back In Anger'.

When Charles Doran's touring company came to Derby in productions of Shakespeare my father used to invite him and some of the cast back to our house after the performance. As a child I used to sit in my pyjamas on the top step of the stairs and listen to the sounds of the party drifting up from below. Ralph Richardson came frequently and, years later, when I was with a production at the Savoy Theatre, I wrote to him, reminding him of this, and got a charming letter back.

I made my stage debut aged eight in the school production of 'The Frogs of Aristophanes' as one of the Frog Chorus. My first words on any stage were

> "Brek kek kek kek koax koax
> Koax as we grow in the mire"

As I crouched in the wings waiting for my cue, dressed in my frog costume, (it was so made that I couldn't stand up in it), I noticed that my yellow cotton chest was heaving up and down. I could hardly breathe because of a mixture of excitement and stage fright. But there wasn't anywhere else in the world where I'd rather have been at that moment. Later on, in my junior school I played the leading part in J M Barrie's 'A Kiss for Cinderella'. I think that my performance surprised my father. My mother used to infuriate me, years later by saying, after she'd seen me in a professional production "Yes, but you've never been so good again as you were as Cinderella".

As I grew up I sometimes played small parts in the Shakespeare Society's annual production, among them Moth in 'A Midsummer Night's Dream' and The Prince of Wales in 'Richard III'. Apparently I was thought to have acted well as the Prince but, later on, had to endure a lot of criticism from the family when I played Titania. During the rehearsals I had suffered from the fact that I had had two directors, the official one and my mother. But I've always considered Titania to be a particularly demanding part.

Rona Laurie os as the Prince of Wales in Richard III

Our family consisted of four girls, one of them being my identical twin Joan. We looked so alike that up to the age of eighteen our own parents couldn't tell us apart when we were asleep. However, we were quite different in temperament, had different friends at school and after we left, our lives went in completely opposite directions. Joan only recently gave up gardening. I was always very close to my father and I believe that I took the place of the son he never had. I went on fishing trips with him to Norfolk and Devon and I remember fishing for pike on the Broads, sitting in a boat on a freezing day and being fortified by a slug of neat whisky and a raw onion. Years later I developed a taste for whisky and small cigars. Going back to my hotel after a gruelling day's adjudicating at a speech and drama festival, I would sit up in bed smoking a cigar and sipping a single malt whisky. When I told this to Professor John Holgate, one of my colleagues at the Guildhall School of Music and Drama, he murmured, "Yes, you are fortunate in being able to enjoy both the masculine and feminine sides of your character".

We children loved our father's wit and he used to regale us with stories of his life as a medical student at Edinburgh University where his father had also been. I remember my grandfather also telling me how he had been tutored by Dr. Bell whom Conan Doyle, a class-mate, used as a model for Sherlock Holmes. Dr. Bell was famous for his powers of deduction. When my father was a freshman he was flattered to be cast by the University Dramatic Society for their coming production of a classical play. When he asked what part he was being given, he was told "a Greek whore". He was slim with a mop of fair curls in those days.

We had a very happy childhood. This, of course, was in the days before television and there was much more imaginative play among children than there is today. We created imaginary characters and improvised themes around them, for example, The Creeper family, consisting of Lord Creeper, Lady Creeper and their daughter Virginia. (This anticipated Humphrey Lyttelton's radio show 'I'm Sorry I Haven't A Clue'). I played his lordship, my twin, her ladyship while our younger sister Pauline doubled the parts of

Virgina and their little mulatto maid, Prilla, (political correctness was unknown then.) We used another set of characters drawn from stories of Robin Hood. I played Robin of course; Joan was Maid Marian and Pauline Friar Tuck. She was a plump child and we dressed her in an old brown woollen dressing gown, much too big for her, with the pockets, appropriately stuffed with sweets and with medical supplies stolen from our father's surgery. He was cast as the villain, King John, and sometimes took part in our games. On one humiliating occasions, Robin, the leader of the band, had to be rescued by him from the tallest tree in the garden, having been wedged between two branches.

One Christmas we were given a set of Red Indian costumes, those of a Brave, a Squaw and a Papoose. They were made of cheap brown cotton and were highly flammable. One day I was nearly burnt to death when I fell, wearing my Indian costume between the fire guard and the gas fire in the day nursery. I can still remember my terror. I lay a few inches from the flames until I was rescued by our nurse. I can't remember our parents ever being told about it.

We were taken at Christmas to the pantomime at the Grand Theatre. 'Robinson Crusoe' is the one which stands out most vividly in my mind. It starred Randolph Sutton, billed as 'Britain's only male principal boy'. After the interval, during which, supposedly, he had been wrecked on the desert island the curtain rose on a transformation scene, a beach surrounded by a semi-circle of large oyster shells, each one holding a beautiful native girl, who one after another, stepped out onto the strand. The climax was reached when the last shell, which was the largest, slowly opened. It was lined with white satin and lit by electric lights and out stepped Robinson Crusoe dressed in a white leather doublet, tights and thigh length white leather boots. He walked down to the footlights to the accompaniment of the orchestra playing "Ah, Sweet Mystery of Life, At Last I've Found Thee", we children, who were in a box, screamed with delight. But, even at that age, I felt that there was something odd about it. Randolph Sutton was a popular musical hall artiste. His best known song was 'On Mother Kelly's Doorstep'. In this pantomime I remember he sang, 'When the red, red robin comes bob, bob, bobbing along', 'Give Yourself a Pat on the Back' and 'Is Mister Izzy In? Is He? Is He?'

We didn't only invent names for the characters in our games but also for our toys and our pet. We had a large rag doll whom we christened Nellie Peggy Millhouse Laurie. Millhouse was our nurse's name. One summer evening when our parents were giving a cocktail party in the drawing room which was directly under the night nursery, we threw her out of the window, that is the doll. She was dressed in one of Pauline's blue and white gingham frocks. The guests were horrified to see what they thought was a small child falling past the window. They rushed out to see her sprawled on the gravel, apparently lifeless. We were severely punished for that prank. The family pet was a Dutch barge-dog which one of our father's grateful patients, Mrs Coeshot, had given us. She was a breeder of pedigree dogs and this one was the smallest of the litter and couldn't be shown. He looked like a cross between a Chow and a Pomeranian. We adored him and christened him Admiral Bonzo Togo Coeshot Laurie. Admiral Togo was a Japanese naval commander much in the news at the time. Bonzo was the name of a strip-cartoon character. The dog was devoted to our father and used to wait for him every afternoon, ready to escort him across the road after he had finished work at the Derbyshire Royal Infirmary. Bonzo would go across to meet him. One day I had a traumatic experience when I saw the dog in the middle of the road, right in the path of a lorry which ran over him. But, by a miracle, all six wheels missed him and he emerged unscathed and continued calmly across to the other side.

At that time there was a paperback series of 'The Adventures of Robin Hood' and another one featuring the private detective Sexton Blake and his assistant Tinker. My father was an avid reader of both. I was sometimes sent into the newsagents to buy the latest editions while he waited in the car outside. I suppose he felt that it was beneath his dignity as a consultant to be known as a reader of such fiction.

My twin and I were fortunate in the boarding school chosen for us. We were sent to Penrhos College when we left Derby High

School. I was lucky enough to have an inspired, if somewhat eccentric, drama teacher, Ethel Barber. She used to enter her private pupils for the grade examinations of the Guildhall School of Music and Drama and for its Teaching Diploma. She also coached me for the Performers Diploma of the Royal Academy of Music. I took the latter in my last year at school - and failed. My mother, not known for her tact, woke me up the morning that the result came through to tell me the news. I subsequently entered myself for it when I was on the staff at the Guildhall School. Little did I know that when I took those early Guildhall examinations that I should one day become Head of Drama in Education and of the Post-Graduate Course.

Miss Barber cast me as St. Joan in the end of term production of a one-act play 'The Vision at the Inn'. I loved the part and achieved some local fame when a photograph of me in chain armour, kneeling and clutching a sword, with a holy expression on my pudgy face was displayed in the Colwyn Bay's photographer's shop window. Another member of the staff was Miss Brandenberg, who taught us German. She was tall and well-built with flaxen hair. Her idol, Adolf Hitler would have approved of her Aryan looks. She used to talk with great enthusiasm and shining eyes about "Our Führer's" inspiring speeches to the nation. She was very popular with us and her class composed a song and sang it to her in German on her birthday.

One day as I was sitting in my study, a privilege given to six-formers, there was a knock on the door and a diminutive figure in a kilt was ushered in. It was the Scottish variety artist Sir Harry Lauder. He was in Colwyn Bay visiting his White Heather home. Earlier he had been entertaining us with some of his famous songs 'I Love a Lassie', 'Will ye stop yer tickling Jock' and 'Roamin' in the Gloamin'. He ended the impromptu concert by saying, "Now you've had enough for nothing". He had a reputation for meanness. We lined the drive cheering to see him off. One term the Comedie Française came to perform for us. I was greatly impressed by the accomplished technique of this famous company.

During the war Penrhos College was moved from Colwyn Bay to make room for the Ministry of Food and was re-located in

Derbyshire in the stately house of Chatsworth. My youngest sister, Pat, was a pupil there for five and a half happy years. It had a near miss when a pilot, returning from an air-raid, flew over it spraying the lawn with machine-gun bullets. Luckily the girls were ten minutes late coming out of doors after their evening meal and no one was hurt, but the walls were chipped and a bullet went through one of the chairs in the staff-room, luckily unoccupied at the time.

Throughout my childhood and school days I had kept the flame of my ambition to become an actress alight and now I was ready for the next stage of my education, before I was allowed to go to drama school.

Rona Laurie as St. Joan

UNIVERSITY. The Dramatic Society

W hen I left Penrhos my father asked me what I wanted to do; "Go to drama school of course". He agreed, providing I got some qualification before entering such a precarious (or "procurious" as one of my later students once called it) profession. It was thought that a Batchelor of Arts degree in English Literature might be helpful to me in my chosen profession. I wanted to go to Oxford, but at that time Latin and Mathematics were required subjects for entrance. As these were my two weakest it was out of the question. However, I was offered a place in the Honours English School at Birmingham University and, although I didn't realise it at the time, this was very fortunate for me. The English Department, and particularly the Honours School, was then one of the finest in the country. The faculty possessed a number of distinguished professors, headed by Ernest de Sélincourt and A.M.D. Hughes. I had the latter as my tutor and also Helen Gardner before she went to Oxford to become the Merton Professor of English Literature. And for a short time I had her friend, Elsie Duncan-Jones, an authority on the poet Marvell. Our lecturer in Classics was Louis MacNeice, the poet. He had the thankless task of coaching the first year Honours under-graduates in Latin. He was tall and thin with dark, Spanish-looking features and a haughty, sardonic expression. Not surprising, when he had to listen to our efforts to translate 'The Iliad'; mine, with the help of a half-concealed crib, which didn't escape comment. I only managed to scrape through the exam in my fourth and final year.

This was an exciting time to be reading English Literature. T.S. Eliot was striking a new note in modern poetry and we students responded with enthusiasm. "I have measured out my life with coffee spoons" was often quoted in the Union bars. And we couldn't have had a better coach than Helen, later Dame Gardner, the authority on him. Professor Hughes was not impressed and I remember that in one tutorial he quoted some lines from 'Preludes'. "Call that poetry?" he exclaimed. This was not a typical reaction. He was a small, white-haired man, practically blind. And he had a spiritual quality. One of his students used to say "When Professor Hughes asks one to open the window, one goes to it like a knight in shining armour, in search of the Holy Grail". It was always a shock to his first-year students attending his lecture on 'Hamlet' to see him walk onto the platform, settle himself behind the lectern, and deliver the first sentence with astonishing, fierce intensity "Now I could drink blood".

In my first term I joined the Dramatic Society (B.U.D.S) and was soon deeply involved in its activities both as a director and actress. During the rehearsals for my production of 'Much Ado About Nothing' the student playing Hero became ill and I took over her part at short notice. And I was cast in George Bernard Shaw's 'Back to Methuselah '. This was a big challenge. In my final year I played Portia in 'The Merchant of Venice'. My mother came over from Derby to see the show and sent a note round to me in the interval; "You are wearing too much rouge and your ears are showing". This was of course, meant well, but was hardly encouraging in the middle of a performance. Dorothy Reynolds was a prominent member of the Society and went on to play leading parts in the West End, including the matron in Alan Bennett's 'Habeas Corpus' and she collaborated with Julian Slade in the long-running musical 'Salad Days'. Another member was Henry Reed who wrote arguably the best poem to come out of the second world war, 'Naming of Parts', and a much anthologised parody of Eliot called 'Chard Willow'.

> "As we get older we do not get any younger.
> Seasons return and today I am fifty-five
> And this time last year I was fifty-four"

He and I appeared together in the University's Carnival Review at the Prince of Wales Theatre. It was directed by

R. D. Smith who was to become the legendary innovative producer for the BBC's Drama Department. The pianist was John Barber, afterwards the theatre critic for the Sunday Times. Henry and I were in a sketch together. He wasn't popular with the rugger-playing 'hearties' and the night when they were in the audience they pelted the stage with fruit and vegetables during our sketch. I believe that they were only directed at Henry in his Noel Coward-style silk dressing gown. Afterwards, the manager of the theatre came round in a great state to my dressing room to apologise but apparently I took it very calmly. I think that I must have learnt resilience from my father who expected us not to make a fuss when he teased us. Whether acting or directing I thoroughly enjoyed my time with B.U.D.S.. After rehearsals we would all go to the pub and I remember once seeing W.H. Auden there looking like a golden-haired cherub. It was, of course, long before his face became so wrinkled that he himself said that it was like "a wedding-cake that had been left out in the rain".

It was while I was up at university that I made my debut onto the professional stage. Derek Salzburg was putting on 'Mr. Wu' in his Alexandra Theatre. I was given the non-speaking part of a Chinese girl. I remember that the play began with me tossing a ball to Chinese Girl Number Two uttering strange, Chinese sounding words in pidgin English which I had to improvise. I used to study the Middle English text set for the Honours English course in the dressing room, much to the bewilderment of my fellow actress.

I graduated in the summer of 1938. It wasn't until the end of my stage career when I got the post of a lecturer in English Literature with particular reference to drama at the Guildhall School at the salary of one guinea an hour that I fully realised what a tremendous advantage my four years at Birmingham had been and in fact still is now that I have a private practice coaching students on audition speeches for drama schools and for speech and drama examinations. I particularly enjoyed our specialist period on the course. It was the Romantics, and with de Sélincourt and Hughes, the acknowledged authorities on Wordsworth and Shelley respectively, we were well-served.

And then, apart from dramatic society productions the social life was stimulating, to say the least, particularly for we girls who were outnumbered by the men and in demand as partners at dances and hops. I made no close friends in my year but made up for it by the number of boyfriends I collected from other faculties, for example those of medicine, civil engineering and mining. Tony Cowgill was a year ahead of me and on the Mining Course. At the ages of 90 and 91 respectively we renewed our acquaintance. He was still working in the business world, and was Director of the British Management Data Foundation. He employed two secretaries and made frequent visits to London to chair business meetings. During the war he rose to the rank of Brigadier. He reminded me of the time when he took me to see a film about the Bengal Lancers in which my heart-throb Gary Cooper appeared. Apparently I ticked him off for his extravagance in paying two and sixpence each for our seats in the balcony. Then there were Monty and David, both on the Civil Engineering course, and Philip who was reading Geography. He was killed at Anzio Beach Head. James was a medical student. Their names frequently figured in my diaries after I came down from Birmingham. But that was yet to come. Now, in August, 1938 I was off for a holiday in the Isle of Skye.

Rona Laurie at the Guildhall School of Music and Drama

HOLIDAYS. Over the Sea To Skye

We had a family house in Broadford in the south of Skye (it is now a hotel) and used to spend our summer holidays there. Mimi was proud of her Highland ancestry. She came from the Ross clan and we children wore kilts of the Ross hunting tartan in the summer. Her father was James Ross, known as Hamish Ruhr, the Gaelic for red-haired James. There is a monument 'erected to the memory of James Ross, Broadford, Skye, by his many friends and acquaintances as a token of their esteem. 1845-1902'.

Our father came from Lowland stock and, although she never mentioned it, it was tacitly understood by we children that she regarded this as a disadvantage. I can still remember one of my sisters saying "We have three Scottish grandparents and one English one" to which we chorused "Yes, but Granny can't help it."

That summer was unusually fine for Skye, with much less rain. There is a local saying "When you can't see across the Loch it is raining, and when you can it means that it's going to rain". It was before the bridge was built from the mainland and people could still quote:

> 'Speed bonny boat like a bird on the wing
> On with the sailors cry
> Carry the lad who was born to be King
> Over the sea to Skye,'

The lad being Prince Charles Edward Stuart, Bonnie Prince Charlie.

Although we were lucky with the weather that summer we could not escape that pest of the Western Highlands, the midges. Nothing seemed able to keep them at bay, not sprays, not anti-midge preparations such as citronella, not cigarette smoke. I have never forgotten the itching irritation of their bites and the red lumps they raised. The local minister, the Reverend Hector McLean lived in the manse just down the road from our house. He had four sons, Hugh, Willy, Alastair and Curdy. Willy and Alastair were medical students. They took us, that is my twin, younger sister Pauline and cousin Eleanor to dances, hops and ceilidhs and to excursions round the island. One of their friends had a boat and we went on fishing trips. August is the season of the Highland Games and that year we went to the ones at Portree and Isle Ornsay and to the dances afterwards. On the 15th August we had a picnic in the rain and I found a sprig of lucky white heather. The next day Alastair and I went for a ten mile tramp and started to explore the Cuillin Hills, but somehow missed seeing Loch Coruisk, the famous 'Black Loch'.

Our house was at the mouth of a small river which ran into Broadford Bay. On the 20th my diary entry was "The sea was very rough but I had a lovely bathe in the breakers". Later, I went for a long walk in the rain with Alastair. We sheltered in a shepherd's hut and he said he wanted to marry me. On the Sunday our family went to church. My sisters and I bathed afterwards but as one was not supposed to bathe on a Sunday we hid our costumes under our clothes and wore them soaking wet coming back. Alastair and I went fishing and lost an anchor. We were swept out into the bay, washed up on the island of Pabay and had to be rescued by launch. On the 24th I noted that it poured with rain all day. I had tea and dinner at the Sligachan Hotel and then went on to a dance at Isle Ornsay. This was great fun and was followed by a ceilidh at Mary B McLean's house. She was a popular singer in Skye and a favourite song of hers was:

> 'Way up in Clachan with Dougal McEachen
> Oh I was as happy as happy could be…'

I had the temerity to sing this at one or two parties, but only when well-lubricated.

On the 26th a lovely hot day, Alastair, Willy and my cousin Eleanor and I climbed the hill behind the village, Ben Na Caillach, the Hill of the Old Woman. On the way up I bathed naked in a tarn apparently unobserved. The next day Alastair and I visited a marble quarry. He told me that he was in love with me. I didn't record my reaction, but my last entry for that day was "Skye is almost unbearably beautiful".

The old rhyme

"Jerusalem, Athens and Rome
I would see before I die
But I'd rather not see
Any one of the free
Than be exiled forever from Skye"
expressed my feelings exactly.

On the Sunday we went to church and for a walk afterwards. There was a lovely full tide. The next day I sang at a ceilidh. I must have been a little tight because I haven't got a singing voice, and even have difficulty in keeping in tune.

We left Skye on September the 3rd and crossed over to Kyleakin by the Kyle of Lochalsh ferry. In 2007 Skye ceased to be called an island because the Highland Council decided it should drop its 'Anglican, slavish name' in favour of the Gaelic Eilena Cheo. This means the "Isle of Mist". I wonder how non-Gaelic speakers cope with this pronunciation. In fact, they don't have to; the general public persists in calling the island Skye.

And so the holiday ended. I was, as always, sad at leaving but there was the exciting prospect of my audition at the Royal Academy of Dramatic Art ahead.

❀IV❀
1938

RADA - The Dream Is Realised

When I got back to Derby I started to rehearse my audition speeches. I had my hair shampooed (three and sixpence) and bought some new shoes (seven shillings). It is hard now to imagine the cost of hairdressing and clothes. Life at home was difficult because of the attitude of my mother. She was very worried about my determination to become a professional actress. I can see now why the sight of my turning down the proposals I was getting from eligible young men infuriated her. One of my diary entries reads "Had an awful evening with Mimi. I could have screamed." I remember her saying to me "Most young girls want to get married and have a family, but you're not like that, are you Rona?" Years later when I read the following passage in the American playwright Moss Hart's autobiography entitled 'Act One' I felt that it explained my mother's and sisters' reactions to my commitment to a stage career.

"It is noticeable, I think, that anyone who has tasted the heady wine of the theatre, even in the most menial of its jobs, is cut off from the outside world forever after. The world of the theatre is as closed a tribe and as removed from the civilian world as a gypsy encampment and those who enter it are spoiled for anything else for the rest of their lives."

And I also identified myself with Laurence Olivier's remark "Acting is like the first sip of beer, the one you probably stole as a child, the taste you never forget." Although not a beer-drinker, I can understand this. Only my father seemed able to imagine what motivated me and could cross the barrier between me and the rest of the family. He once said to me "I realise that this is your life Rona". On the 21st September I went up to London to audition for RADA.

My diary entry was "I took the test alright I think." Afterwards David, one of my university boyfriends, took me for tea at the Royal Empire Society. On the 22nd I heard that I had been accepted by RADA but I hadn't got a scholarship. On the 27th I recorded "War is terribly close, but I can't feel anything." We got fitted with gas masks. On October the 8th I started my first term at the Academy.

In the late thirties and forties RADA students were exceptionally lucky in their tutors. Some of them were beyond the call up age and for others this had been extended. All of them were either practising actors or actresses or had established reputations as Directors. And so from the first we students were given a realistic view of what life would be like when we entered the profession and were given advice on how to set about getting work and finding an agent. Most helpfully they told us how to cope with the inevitable periods of being out of work, or "resting".

I was a year or two older than the rest of my class and I believe that this was an advantage because it meant that I had a more serious attitude to the training than some of my fellow students. Alan Badel who was in my year was only sixteen. Madame Gachet, his tutor, said that he was the most brilliant student that she had ever taught. Later he was to play The Fool in 'King Lear', one of his many successful parts. At the end of the course I was awarded the medal for good studentship. When I went to Gower Street for a meeting a few years ago I saw my name on the honours board in the hall. I was gratified to see that the one which followed it was that of the actor Ronald Pickup. I would have preferred a date not to have been given though.

Now that I was well and truly launched on a stage career my earliest dream was fulfilled. On that first morning there was a role-call. This produced one or two surprises. The name 'Pansy Priest' was called out. It never appeared again. One well-endowed student's father was an executive of a big dairy organisation. I've forgotten her name, but her nickname was United Dairies.

It took us a little time to settle down. We were given mysterious instructions such as "Act with your toenails". We did our best to comply. A few of the girls in that first term seemed to regard the Academy as some sort of finishing school. Some of them were in society and boasted about being "at RADA". The rumour went round that only girls of this class were accepted for the course and the so called "RADA voice" was ridiculed. These false impressions were soon dissipated by the high standard of acting in the school's public performances.

On October the 13th I read the part of Mrs. Candour in Sheridan's late eighteenth-century Comedy of Manners 'The School for Scandal'. I have always thought that this was a bad choice for first year students. We had neither the vocal technique to cope with the demands of the dialogue nor the experience to manage the movement, gesture and manners of high society. And we had no idea how to handle the accessories of the period, the fans, canes, snuff-boxes and swords. Nor did we realise the effect that the costume would have on our movement. Our Director, Stella Patrick-Campbell, daughter of the famous actress Mrs. Patrick Campbell was familiar with the hallowed traditions associated with the original production at Drury Lane theatre in 1777 and which had been faithfully followed by directors ever since. I have a vivid memory of her screaming at poor Austin Coates, son of the composer Eric, at the dress rehearsal when he produced a letter from his waistcoat pocket instead of from the back-pocket of his breeches, which was the traditional piece of business. Though how he could have been expected to know this I couldn't imagine. She told the story of how on the first night of the original production the Lady Sneerwell fluffed her first line and said "The snakes, Mr. Paragraph you say were all inserted" instead of "The paragraphs you say Mr. Snake were all inserted." Our Lady Sneerwell exclaimed "Oh I wish you hadn't told me that, I am sure that I will be so nervous on the first night that I'll make the same mistake." From reading my diary I realised that the part of Mrs Candour was giving me trouble. However, on the 4th October I noted that the way I read the epilogue in the character of Lady Teazle was thought to be the best in the class.

We had three talks that term, one from the Principal Sir Kenneth Barnes, one from J.B. Priestly and one from the actor and director

E. Martin Browne. We took advantage of the fact that the West End is only a short distance from Gower Street and of the cheap theatre tickets. You could get a seat in the gallery for two shillings at most theatres, and for sixpence at the Old Vic. Programmes cost from three to sixpence. Stools were provided for the queues waiting for the doors to open and these were often entertained by buskers. Among the plays that I saw that term were Dodie Smith's 'Dear Octopus' starring John Gielgud and Marie Tempest and St John Irvine's 'Robert's Wife' with Edith Evans in the main part.

I was thoroughly enjoying my first term and wrote in the diary, "Life is good, good, good. I don't want my time here to end." After my somewhat trying time as Mrs Candour, I was delighted to be cast as Rosalind in 'As You Like It', our next production. I felt that this sun-lit comedy was a much more suitable choice for our class than 'The School for Scandal' had been, and I apparently developed the character well in rehearsal. But I was still finding Mrs Candour very difficult and was depressed about my acting ability. However, I was greatly cheered at the end of term because one of our tutors, Winifred Oughton said that Alan MacNaughtan and I were two of the most promising students she'd ever coached. Alan fulfilled his promise by winning the Academy's Gold Medal and enjoyed a successful career on the stage. It was not all hard work that term. I enjoyed some welcome weekend breaks. Most of us were living in lodgings approved by the Academy - mine were in King Henry's Road, Swiss Cottage. But some students commuted from the Home Counties. I was sometimes invited by Tony Previté, a classmate, to Osney Lodge, his parent's home near Maidenhead. My sole comment after my first weekend there was "Lovely bath in a lovely bathroom. But luxury isn't everything." My struggle with Mrs Candour continued. After one rehearsal I wrote "I must get my movement better." The dress rehearsal was not too good but the performance on November the 1st went well. Obviously the costumes and make-up helped. And so my first term at RADA ended and I went home to Derby. My childhood dream was becoming a reality and I couldn't wait to begin my second term.

MY SOCIAL LIFE. "Your Love Affairs Are In A Hopeless Tangle"

During the holidays I kept working at my RADA acting assignments and on voice production and speech exercises. Our tutor was the distinguished voice-teacher Iris Warren. She said "Find your own voice" to each of us. When I was practising at home I didn't get much encouragement from my sisters, who used to stand outside my bedroom door and mimic my efforts. But I didn't care.

In our second term increasing demands were made on us to acquire secure physical and vocal techniques. As Laurence Olivier once remarked, "Talent is very plentiful, but skill is rather rare." When I went back to London I found the war-time atmosphere oppressive. Recently I have seen the film 'Mrs. Henderson Presents'. This celebrated her management of the Windmill Variety Theatre. Throughout the war it never failed to put on a show. It proudly proclaimed "We Never Closed." Judi Dench was excellent as Mrs. Henderson. There was a scene in particular which brought back memories. It showed a crowded dance floor with the Forces on leave. British, American, Polish and French moving slowly round to the strains of Ray Noble's 'Good Night Sweetheart'. Bands used to play this for the last dance of the evening at wartime hops. It became almost the signature tune of Al Bowly and was even more popular than 'We'll Meet Again' and 'There'll Be Bluebirds Over the White Cliffs of Dover' as sung by Vera Lynn, the Force's Sweetheart. Another popular song of the period was 'These Foolish Things'; the lyrics were charming and inventive and I loved the tune. I used to hear the night-club entertainer Leslie A. Hutchinson

(Hutch) sing it at the Savoy hotel, flourishing a white handkerchief long before Pavarotti used his as his trademark, and on one of my wartime tours it was played by the live orchestra in the pit every night before the curtain went up. Another of Hutch's songs was 'What is This Thing Called Love? This Funny Thing Called Love.' I could certainly have asked this question in view of my numerous boyfriends in wartime London. Another vivid memory was Ivy Benson's All Girls Band. She used to come into my local pub in between sessions at the Cumberland Hotel. At first she had a struggle to be accepted, but eventually found success and took the band overseas to entertain the troops.

But now back to my story and the beginning of 1939. By mid-January I was itching to return to London for the new term which started on the 19th. I hadn't got the double-remove that I'd hoped for, but there were compensations. We had a new tutor, John Fernald, a well-known West End director, who later became the Principal of RADA. He made a big impression on the girls in my group, especially on me. "Very attractive" I wrote in my diary. He was indeed remarkably good-looking. He was not the only tutor on whom I had a student crush when I was at RADA. The chosen play that term was George Bernard Shaw's 'Arms And the Man'. I was cast as Louka, the maid. I was not enthusiastic about this. However, in the other production 'Twelfth Night' I got the part of one of the Violas. As there are so few female parts in Shakespeare, they had to be shared. But, I was lucky enough to be given the scene in which Viola, dressed as the page Cesario woos Olivia on behalf of Orsino. It has the wonderful 'willow cabin' speech in it.

> 'Make me a willow cabin at your gate,
> And call upon my soul within the house,
> Write loyal cantons of contemned love.'

We were worked very hard that term. A typical day began at nine-thirty and didn't finish until seven with only a one hour break at lunchtime. In addition Fernald had asked me to be his stage manager for 'Arms and The Man'. On the 25th we had a talk from Robert Atkins about the Open Air Theatre in Regent's Park which he managed. He was rather depressing about our futures in the theatre but gave us three pieces of advice. "One, save; Two, don't drink; Three, don't smoke." On January the 26th I heard that Fernald was married. This was a blow but I tried to cheer myself up, I wrote "My looks are improving I think, but I am going to make myself far prettier. I am pegging away at the old hair!" Mercifully, that was the only example of a 'jolly hockey-sticks style' that I found in the diaries.

I made the most of the opportunities we had to see West End Productions and the latest pictures on release. David took me to see 'Algiers'. The diary comments were "Film not very good, but Charles Boyer has plenty of Latin feeling and slumberous fire in Pepe Le Moko. On the 29th I saw Noel Coward's 'Design for Living'. The stars were Diana Wynyard who "acted well" and Rex Harrison "very much at ease." February the 6th brought another blow, when I heard that Fernald had been married <u>twice</u>. 'What is This Thing called Love' could have been the leit motif of my social life during those years, with my suitors constantly declaring their devotion. David was especially persistent. On February the 9th the entry was "Dinner with David in Soho. We had trout and wine. The meal cost him two and sixpence a head." Afterwards we went to a film and he put his arm around me. "How boring men can be."

Another of my boyfriends was Teddy Obolensky, the younger brother of Prince Alexander who is famous for his spectacular tries against the All Blacks at Twickenham in 1936. I had known both of them from my schooldays in Derby. The medical fraternity was a close-knit group and my sister and I were often asked around to a local G.P. Dr Patey's house. Alex and Teddy often spent their school holidays with the Patey family. Alex used to coach us and the Patey children, George and Dora, in rugby strategy. He would station us at staggered intervals across the lawn and challenge us to tackle him as he ran with the ball, weaving from one end of the lawn to the other. I always felt partly responsible for the famous try which the Morning Post described thus: "Runners we have seen before, but never such a runner with such an innate idea of where to go and how to get there. His double swerve to gain his first try was remarkable enough, but the extraordinary turn-in and diagonal right-to-left run which won him the second... will never be forgotten by anybody who saw it." He used to down a dozen oysters before a big game with Oxford University. He was killed while he was training as an RAF pilot when his Hurricane crashed in an accident. He is now commemorated by a statue in Ipswich.

Teddy took me out frequently that term. Once we went to his actress friend Oriel Ross's flat for drinks. A Lord somebody (tame snake) was there. I was not impressed. First we had supper at Brasserie Universelle, then went to see the show at the Prince of Wales Theatre and finished at the Troika Club before he took me home in a taxi.

On the 13th February disaster struck. I developed mumps and on the next day was in considerable pain. What a way to celebrate St. Valentine's Day! However, I resolved to spend my enforced absence from the Academy by having a home beauty treatment and doing some chores. I washed my angora jersey - it looked like a skinned rabbit, and I bought a bottle of Innoxa complexion milk (three and sixpence.) After a week in bed, on the Sunday before going back to RADA, I went to the City Temple to hear the charismatic Leslie Weatherhead preach on 'missions'. 27th February first day back. I felt depressed because I wasn't used in any of the classes. But the following day, which was gruelling, made up for it. I had a bad class on gesture, with our movement tutor Annie Fligg, but got it right in the end. I had a drink in the evening with the faithful David. "It's damnable that I can't get a kick out of his devotion." March 1st Rehearsed Viola's duel scene. "It's devilish hard."

March 13th - Went to the Vic Wells Ball. John Gielgud and Michael Redgrave were the judges of the Best Costume Competition. According to my diary I approved of Redgrave who was "natural and unaffected", but not of Gielgud who "posed all evening in a statuesque attitude" wearing a blue silk down-to-the-ground cloak. I seemed to have been in a particularly critical mood just then because I described the acting as bad in Dorothy Sayer's play 'Busman's Honeymoon'. "Basil Foster was quite wrong as Lord Peter Wimsey and so was the actress who played Harriet." March 18th

- The dress rehearsal of 'Twelfth Night' went well and I had a good make-up with my hair in a page-boy bob. That evening I saw Patrick Hamilton's 'Gas Light'. To the Temple again on the Sunday. Weatherhead preached a powerful sermon on "the consolation of forgiveness". 20th March - First performance of Twelfth Night. One of our tutors Miss Carrington said that it was an exceptional show for first year students. On the 29th we had a morning rehearsal of 'Arms and the Man' and I went on a search for props in the afternoon and had an infuriating time at Clarkson's about the type of revolver we wanted (d-inefficiency). The second dress rehearsal went smoothly and the opening show that evening was grand. Mimi came up from Derby to see it. I thought that I played Louka quite well but she was very dampening about my performance and make-up. I went with her to the Cumberland Hotel and then back to my digs. "But I will act well one day, despite her criticism."

The following day I went to Leichner's, the stage make-up shop to buy some more grease-paint. This was the kind of make-up we used in those days. The foundation was two sticks. They were known by numbers, five and nine being the most popular for women. Carmine Two was used for the lips and cheeks and we put a dot of red in the corner of the eyes and in the nostrils. We must have looked like rocking-horses. I was told that I had to look middle-aged and heavily made up as Mrs. Candour. I must have used nearly half a stick of Carmine Two. The lashes were thickened by "spit black". This was a little cake of solid black mascara some of which was put on a metal spoon and held over a candle-flame to melt. It was applied with a small brush or, more often, with a bent hair pin. The result was stiff spikes. Wet White was put on the hands and arms. The men used spirit gum to secure their beards, goatees, moustaches and side-burns. This did not always prove reliable. Once, when I was playing opposite Ernest Milton on tour in a Victorian melodrama, I had a traumatic experience. Ernest was an American actor who had come to England and he became one of the great interpreters of 'Hamlet'. Alec Guinness said that he had seen nine Hamlets but he thought that Milton was the greatest. I was very excited at playing opposite such a distinguished man. I was of course very nervous on the first night. My confidence was not helped by being told by the manager of the company Hubert saying, when I was in my dressing room just preparing to make my first entrance, "We should have got a well-known actress for your part." Ernest had been very temperamental during rehearsals and I felt that he shared Hubert's view. One night, as Ernest was preparing to make a dramatic exit, he swung his cloak round and the hook caught in the table-runner and was whirled in the air, dislodging half of his moustache. He misjudged the height of the door as he exited, his top-hat got jammed down over his eyes, and he lost the second half of his moustache. I had the greatest difficulty in keeping a straight face.

Young actresses and actors used to keep their make-up in tin boxes fitted with layers, but the old hands used to make do with a battered cigar-box. A few years ago I was at Chichester Festival Theatre and after the show went backstage to see Alan Badel's daughter Sarah. There on her dressing-table was an old-fashioned tin make-up box with a message from Alan wishing her good luck stuck on the lid.

On the last day of the month I was evidently in high-spirits. This euphoric mood was short-lived however when I was called for a movement rehearsal with Annie Fligg but never used.

April 2nd - "Saw the picture, 'Three Smart Girls' with George Patey"

The next day David took me to see 'The Dawn Patrol'.

As my second term ended, I felt that I needed a break. The invitation to spend a few days with the classmate from my Derby High School days, Pamela came just at the right time. Her father was the Vicar at Urchfont, a village near Devizes in Shropshire.

6th April - "Caught the 2:45 from Paddington to Devizes where she met me in her little car."

We managed to cram the Wylie Valley point-to-point, a dance in Bath Assembly Rooms and the Hunter Trials at Melksham into that weekend.

11th April - "Home to Derby"

"Saw the film 'The Young in Heart' featuring Douglas Fairbanks Junior. (Very attractive)

A good report arrived from RADA and John Fernald's comments were especially encouraging. "A very good student, a very good calm stage-manager, with plenty of initiative and a promising actress." Whoopee! I listened in to 'Arms and the Man' on the radio and commented in my diary "I could have played Raina just as well." At this point in my training I was a mixture of over-confidence and insecurity. I have recently been reading the accompanist Gerald Moore's auto-biography, 'Am I Too Loud?' and thought that his description of the artistic temperament was applicable to me.

"The eternal problem for the performer is the settling of his own mental equilibrium, the striking of a mean between self-conceit and self-confidence, between self-satisfaction and a sober valuation of his worth."

Laurence Olivier put the same idea more succinctly. "The difficulty of acting, I've always thought, is finding the right humility towards the work and the right confidence to carry it out." I would have been shocked at that stage in my training if I'd heard his answer to the question, "What are the three most important attributes for an actor to have? Sincerity, sincerity, sincerity. If you can fake that, you can do anything."

6th May - "Over to Birmingham to meet Monty"

He was another of my university friends and had not been called up because he was in a reserved occupation as the manager in a factory making armaments. We went over to Stratford-on-Avon to see 'Othello' in the Memorial Theatre. John Laurie (no relation) did not impress me as the Moor nor did Joyce Bland as Desdemona but I described Alec Clunes's Iago as "very good". His son Martin Clunes is now enjoying a successful career in television.

During April I was out at Dove Cottage a lot, caught some trout and was taught how to fly-fish by Monty. My father was a keen fisherman and had bought this small cottage on the River Dove. It was in Izaak Walton country in Derbyshire. Monty told me that he loved me terribly and asked me if I would marry him in five years' time, when he made some money.

"Saw the film 'If I Were King'. Ronald Colman's voice was charming."

"If I were King
The world I'd give you for a ruby ring
If I were King"

These words resounded around the cinema. Basil Rathbone was excellent as Louis XI.

"Heard Noel Coward's 'The Vortex' on radio."

My first term had more than fulfilled my expectations. Early on I had realised that we were going to have to work very hard and be stretched, the teaching was inspiring and in my second term I seemed able to cope with the increased demands of the training and also with my hectic social life.

❧ VI ☙
1939

LEARNING THE CRAFT

On 9th May I went up to London for the start of the new RADA term. I met Pamela and went to the St Martin's Theatre and sat in the Gods to see 'The Man in Half Moon Street'. Both Leslie Banks and Ann Todd were good - not so the play. On 10th May the first day of term. I was in a good set with most of my friends. We had a talk from Sir Kenneth Barnes. One of our tutors was Henry Cass, a well-known Old Vic and West End director. He gave me Juliet's potion speech from 'Romeo and Juliet'. I could hardly believe it. It is a challenge for every actress. When I finished, he asked me if I had done it before. I hadn't. I wondered if he could help me to get to the top, or would he? On the Sunday, George Patey took me to see the film 'Wuthering Heights'. Laurence Olivier was very good. We had a meal afterwards at Lyon's Brasserie. On the 17th we had a talk from the Bishop of Chichester. "Very broad minded, a dear." On the 18th Cass said that I was very good at Juliet, but must get that "macabre" quality. He told me to watch Bette Davis. In the evening I worked on voice exercises as I was worried about my breathing.

At this point my social life features more and more in my diary, because I met Monty's younger brother Peter, nick-named 'Root'. He was an RAF pilot in the 111 fighter squadron stationed in Northolt flying Hurricanes, the precursors of the Spitfire. He won a DFC and bar during the Battle of Britain, being one of "the few" praised by Winston Churchill in his most famous speech.

On 20th May after a good verse-speaking class, followed by one on fencing, I dashed out to Ruislip for the Air Display and met Root for the first time. I noted that he was "<u>very</u>" attractive. Indeed he was one of the most attractive men I have ever met. I blushed to re-read the following. "I had five large sherries, and went to Root's sitting room with Monty and against my better judgement let him make love to me quite a good deal." The next day I felt awful, had a hangover and was weak as a kitten, had practically no breakfast and felt ill and also remorseful about the night before. Monty called for me at twelve. I pretended that it hadn't happened. "I am not in love with him". 22nd May - Had a good rehearsal with Cass, "I do like him, but not as much as I liked J.F.". 23rd May - Saw the play 'First Stop North' starring Esmond Knight, whom I described as "a bit ham". We had quite a good rehearsal with Cass on the next day. He said my Juliet was "good, but too controlled". When I spoke one of Hero's speeches from 'Much Ado About Nothing' he told me that there was no humour in my voice and asked me if I had a sense of humour. He wanted the speech spoken in the style of eighteenth-century artificial comedy and said that this was difficult. "I'll say it was".

26th May - I was chosen as the representative on the Student Council. I was working hard at "blasted Hero". Went with fellow-students to see Karel Čapek's play 'R.U.R'. Comment, "an infantile, humourless trifle." I must have been in a bad mood. Supper afterwards in Regent's Park. Ian Carmichael brought me back to my digs.

Maidenhead was a popular venue at weekends. That Sunday Monty and Root called for me and after coffee at the Cumberland Hotel we went down to The Bear for lunch and then on to the river. We had great fun sailing although I navigated us into the bank. After a bathe Monty and I returned to The Bear for dinner and afterwards went for a walk in Burnham Beeches. Not for the first time I had to tell him that I wasn't in love with him. I went back to my digs in sober mood. We had a day off from the Academy on Whit Monday. I met Monty for lunch at Northolt and we went sailing again, followed by drinking by the pool at Pinewood and dinner in the RAF mess. Monty told me on the way home that we had better not see each other again. Root phoned that evening and said "You should have broken that off long ago".

Back at RADA the next day. The film-star George Arliss gave us a talk about acting in films. The next time that I rehearsed Juliet's potion speech Cass said "it was good but rather high-pitched." "Will I ever get it right?"

31st May - Supper with David in Regents Park.

June 2nd Got a ticket for the Lyceum Theatre, five and eleven pence, "Good Lord!".

June 3rd - We heard that there was no hope for the ninety-eight men trapped in the Thetis submarine. Special editions all day. I saw the film 'Dark Victory'. Bette Davis played a woman going blind. I can see her now, standing at the top of the stairs and saying, "Have I been a good wife to you?"

June the 5th - Root phoned. I felt ridiculously excited and we were both nervous. On the next day I went with two fellow students to the Theatrical Garden Party. It was a big annual social event, and that year it was held at the Ranelagh Club at Barnes. The President was Noel Coward and it was in aid of the Actors' Orphanage. I have the programme of all the entertainments that were provided. These range from the "All-Sorts of Dogs Show, Ringmaster Lupino Lane" to "Mrs Jarley's Wax-Works" and "Fishing for Fizz". As usual it was supported by a sprinkling of stars, a number of lesser lights and a few drama students. It was a glorious sunny day. Noel Coward resplendent in a morning suit and grey topper was surrounded by fans. We saw Clive Brook, Diana Wynard, Mary Ellis, Diana Churchill and Griffith Jones "incredibly handsome." Anton Walbrook noticed me about to go on the helter-skelter and remarked "You are frightened I think".

We three students were wearing our best flowered summer dresses and smart hats. We ran into John Fernald, who looked very surprised to see us. "You look so nice" he said, shaking us by the hand. Of course, he was used to seeing us in our workaday rehearsal clothes. On June 7th we were introduced to our new tutor. Claud Gurney, an experienced West End Director. I got valuable help watching him coaching the other Juliets in the class. In the evening I saw 'Much Ado About Nothing;' at the Open Air Theatre. Catherine Nesbitt was very good as Beatrice. The Dogberry was too slow. Ducks flew overhead.

The next week began with a dance at Camberley. I apparently drank too much champagne and didn't get to bed until four a.m. when the dawn chorus was in full voice. The remainder of that weekend was spent resting and recuperating. On the Monday Claud Gurney spent the whole of the Shakespeare class coaching me in Juliet's potion speech on the stage. I think that I managed to get some of the horror into it. I shall never forget how he told me to speak the line just before she took the potion

"Romeo, I come, this do I drink to thee".

He said "Imagine that you are going to meet your love and that the sun is coming out".

Money problems were acute. I was dependant on a small monthly allowance, sometimes, as on this occasion, it was late. Everyone seemed to like my Juliet of the day before. Claud Gurney was of course married, but separated from his wife. David took me to The Spaniard's Inn on Hampstead Hill which I did not enjoy very much. I was very friendly with one of my classmates, Elizabeth Sellars. She had a warm voice and a slight Scottish accent. Cass predicted a successful future for her. This was fulfilled as she appeared in several West End Productions, including, John Mortimer's 'A Voyage Round My Father' and 'Tea and Sympathy'. She and I queued on stools for a club performance of Steinbeck's 'Of Mice and Men'. John Mills and Niall MacGinnis gave lovely performances. The last scene was almost unbearably moving and after the curtain fell I couldn't move from my seat while the rest of the audience filed out.

The next week was unusually busy socially. I went down to David's house in Claygate and on the 9th we went to the Aldershot Tattoo. I was greatly impressed by the Guard's drilling. On the way back we had a picnic on the Hog's Back. I had to get up early the next morning to get to London for a verse speaking class. Afterwards George, now a medical student, took me to Chislehurst for St. Bartholomew's Sports Day. Afterwards we saw the film 'Mr. Chips' starring Robert Donat. The day ended with dinner at

The Queen's Hotel. On the 18th David took me to the Mill House for tea. He said he would always be waiting for me, even after I married.

The last day of term was very busy, with classes on mime, voice-production and acting. Elizabeth and I were both waiting for something exciting to happen. We were wanting to meet the 'right man'. There was a cryptic remark in my diary "college boys in Coonskin Coats. I hate them". I can't think what I meant, surely not the boys in our class.

On the 20th I went home to Derby for my twin's wedding in Derby Cathedral to Tinny Thornton. He was a member of my father's cricket club, "The Grasshoppers" and captain of the famous amateur football team 'the Corinthians'. It was a sunny, windy day. Joan looked a dream. Pauline and my cousin Eleanor and I were bridesmaids. Afterwards there was dinner at the Midland Hotel and we ended the day dancing eightsome reels in the marquee set up in our garden.

22nd	I was up early and Pamela drove me back to London.
23rd	There was no trouble at the Academy about my two day's off.

On the Sunday Pamela and I went to Hampton Court. The way into the maze was difficult, but it was easy to find the way out.

26th	Pamela and I went to the Russian Ballet at the Royal Opera House Covent Garden. We saw Irina Baronova in 'The Good-Humoured Ladies' choreographed by Leonide Massine, 'Cinderella' and 'Prince Egor' with choreography by Mikhail Fokine.
22nd	I went to Paul and Bishop and had photographs taken. They said that I had a nice face and photogenic hands (also a double chin).

The month ended on a high note because I was told that the Principal Sir Kenneth had said that I was "very clever, brilliant".

30th	To the Lyceum to see Gielgud's 'Hamlet'. "Incredible, beautiful, simple, deep... I must act and I <u>will</u> one day."
1st July (Saturday)	I still felt dazed by Hamlet and all afternoon in the digs read Hamlet's entire part aloud but couldn't capture John's inflections. He had a deceptive simplicity and I came to the conclusion that the reason why he made it look easy was because he fully understood the meaning of the words and had the technique to convey it to the audience. An actor friend of mine, Trader Faulkner who is a lover of Spain and all things Spanish used the word "duende" and I looked up the definition which is "the ability to transmit a powerfully felt emotion to an audience of strangers with the minimum of fuss and the maximum of restraint". Yes, that was one of the qualities that Gielgud had. I shall always remember the impact he made on his first entrance as Hamlet. Scene: the castle at Elsinore. Flourish of Trumpets. Enter Claudius, King of Denmark, Gertrude, the Queen and counsellors including Polonius and Laertes. There was a pause, and then Hamlet, dressed in a black velvet doublet with a heavy chain entered upstage left and slowly crossed to the down right corner. You could have heard a pin drop.
4th July	I went to the Gate Review at the Ambassador's Theatre and saw a wonderful striptease act.
11th July	Philip, a university friend, picked me up in the evening. We went to Lyon's Corner House and then to the Mayfair Hotel, finishing up at the Embassy Club. The Duke and Duchess of

Kent were there and Rex Harrison and Jim Mollison, the pilot who had married Amy Johnson the famous aviator. There was a wonderful band. I noted. "People stared at me. My frock must have been a success." As Philip and I shuffled round the crowded dance floor, the size of a pocket handkerchief, we came alongside Harrison and his obviously infatuated partner and I distinctly heard him murmur to her, "I <u>am</u> married, you know." Philip got a bit tight and tried to make love to me all evening. "I don't love him".

13th July — The rehearsal of 'Twelfth Night' and my willow-cabin scene as Viola.

14th July — Good rehearsal with Mr. Gurney and then off to Tony Previté's for the weekend. "Their house and gardens are lovely".

The next day we played tennis and in the evening saw the picture 'I Was A Spy' featuring Madeleine Carroll, an alumna of Birmingham University. "She is very beautiful". I left my gloves behind. Yes, we always wore gloves to the pictures then. Those weekends at the Prevités' country house were typical of life in the Home Counties in the thirties and forties. Playwrights used them as the setting for their light comedies. I wouldn't have been surprised if, at any moment during those weekends, a young man in white flannels had burst through the French windows into the drawing room asking enthusiastically, "Who's for tennis?"

July 18th — A good rehearsal with Mr. Gurney. I was working hard at my scene in 'Twelfth Night'. The following Friday some of us went to a sherry party given by a class-mate at Swiss Cottage (Good God!) and then on to a nightclub in Kensington, "rather a mistake". Home at one-thirty a.m.

Tony and I shot off to Maidenhead for another weekend. I had to wear my day-shoes at dinner as I'd forgotten to bring my evening ones. Of course we always changed in the evening. Back to the Academy from Osney Lodge in a Rolls Royce on the Monday for a Shakespeare rehearsal and a test the next day. It was awful to think that there would be no more Shakespeare classes. Went to Oxford for the verse-speaking competition organised by John Masefield the next day. Didn't do well, however I met Christopher Hassell, the actor and poet. "Quite Attractive."

The third term ended on the 26th July and on August the 3rd I drove to Skye with Mimi and Pauline.

❧ VII ☙
1939

RETURN TO SKYE. War is Declared

We had supper en-route to Borough Bridge and a good run the next day as far as Lochearnhead. Mimi was very nervous in the car. I wonder now if she foresaw the accident which we had the next day. As a Highlander she may have had 'second sight'. On the 4th we left Lochearnhead early and reached Crianlarich, then drove round Ballachulish. About three miles south of Tomdown I tried to throw a cigarette out of the sunshine roof. It fell on Pauline's lap and the next thing I knew was that the front wheel on my side went over the edge of the narrow road and the car dropped into the ditch. The steering-wheel broke and gashed my chin and pushed my lower front teeth half-way out of their sockets. Pauline, who was in the back seat, was concussed. Mimi was unhurt and managed to get help. Pauline and I were taken to Inverness Infirmary where I was operated on under a local anaesthetic. My front teeth were pulled out and my chin was stitched. It was very painful indeed. I noted rather pathetically in my diary 'So I won't even be able to have them crowned'.

We had plenty of visitors during the next twelve days. I was nursed well and under the care of a charming Polish doctor, Hanz Lederer. My father was very decent about the accident, but I knew that it was all my fault. Among my visitors was yet another of my Birmingham University friends, Pip Collis. On the 16th August Hanz came to say goodbye and gave me a beautiful spray of peach-coloured gladioli. I can never see them, even to this day without thinking of him and how he helped me through a bad patch. I had been worried all the time about the possibility of my injuries affecting my career. Luckily, they didn't. I had a good dentist at home in Derby. On the 17th Pauline and I resumed our journey to Skye. We went by train from Inverness to the Kyle of Lochalsh, a lovely journey through unbelievably beautiful scenery. Mimi met us off the ferry and we went to Dunan by bus to School House on the loch side Tignamara (our house in Broadford had been let that year). This had a large classroom and a battered old piano. I have vivid memories of the evenings we spent gathered round it to sing. One of our friends came round in the evening. He had quite a good voice and regaled my twin and me with sentimental Victorian ballads, 'I'll Walk Beside You' and 'The Sunshine of Your Smile' gazing soulfully at us. We could hardly keep straight faces.

Alastair came over to welcome us. My diary comment was "I think that I've outgrown him". On the 18th we all went to a concert. Prunella Stack, daughter of the founder of the Women's League of Health and Beauty was there with her husband Lord David Douglas Hamilton, a pilot in the RAF. He was subsequently killed in the war.

19th August	"My articulation is bad but I hope that it improves."
20th August	"Skye calm and quiet with the reflections of the hills in the Loch."
21st August	"We had an excursion over to the island of Raasay on John McLeod's motorboat. We were shown the room Dr. Samuel Johnson had slept in on his tour of the Hebrides. On the way back we fished by the Red Rock and caught fourteen pollock. My share was seven. The hills looked misty and blue and the loch was glassy."
22nd August	"Tea at the Manse"
25th August	"Over to the Kyle of Lochalsh for a dance. We got back to Dunan at six a.m."

On the Sunday I went for a long tramp over the moors by myself.

28th "The glorious sunny weather continued. We bathed in the evening. Alastair came over and we went for a walk along the Old Road. The moon came up; it was magical and we felt bewitched."

29th "Alastair and I went fishing again in Broadford Bay. But we only caught two gurnets in two and a half hours and we got midge-bitten. Later on I bathed in the moonlight by myself."

We had a great adventure on the 30th. Alastair and I set out on our bikes for Torridon and climbed nearly to the top of Blaven, one of the Cuillin range. It was dangerous in places and I got stuck on a rock-face and could move neither up nor down. I was terrified and trembling as Alastair helped me to get safely down. We left Torridon at dusk and rode on our old bikes, without lights for thirteen miles. "Home at eleven p.m. Dead Tired. (No wonder.)"

31st August "Bathed in the evening. The beauty here is unbelievable. And to think that the war might spoil it all."

1st September "Heard that Hitler had sent bombers over Poland. Alastair and I went to the local dance, but felt so depressed that we left early and sat up in the school room till five a.m. I am very fond of him".

2nd September "Over to Armadale to bathe."

Sunday 3rd September "We all went to church. Hector McLean preached a fine sermon. At the end of the service he announced. "War has been declared". "

In the late evening Alastair and I went for a walk and saw that every cottage around the loch had been blacked out. And it didn't look any different from normal. Alastair said "I suddenly realised that I'd been living all my life in a black-out." He stayed with me in the front room until three a.m. and told me that he would marry me if he had the money.

4th September — Packed. Felt terribly depressed all morning. Alastair came in the evening and stayed until two a.m. He was terribly upset and cried.

5th September — Went for a walk. It was windy and starry. Back to Tignamara. We sat up talking until he left at one-thirty a.m. and he said goodbye.

6th September — Left for Derby. Pauline and I were driven to Fort William by Martin, one of our friends. We saw the car - what a mess!

The next day we got as far as Lockerbie and then went on driving in the pouring rain through the Trossachs and Glencoe, until the light went.

8th September — Stopped for tea at Knutsford, then down through Wigan and Warrington. Everything blacked out in Derby.

I have never forgotten that last summer in Skye just before war broke out. In my memory it is bathed in sunlight - the Cuillin Hills, the loch, the sound of the bagpipes coming across the water - the rain - the midges.

9th September — My father and I discussed the possibility of my doing war-work. David came over from Birmingham and we went out to Dove cottage for some fly-fishing. We walked for four miles in slight rain, had tea and then fished. He said he loved me and wanted to marry me, but didn't have enough money to keep in me in silk-stockings.

11th September	Fixed up the black-out for the big window in the drawing-room. Teddy Obolensky, Alex's younger brother arrived. He had been called up and seemed very depressed. He had to go off to Dover for army training on the next day.
13th September	Coffee with Teddy at the Kardomah and then out to the cottage after tea.
14th September	Started work at the canteen and noted that I served fifteen cups of tea. "If only I could be given some real war work." Out to the cottage in the evening. A glorious sunset.
15th September	To the canteen in the morning. Out to the cottage again in the evening. A lovely starry night. Saw a comet.
16th September	Monty came over and we went out to the cottage, me riding on the pillion of his motorbike. We fished on the Sunday. My father came out and delivered a hymn of hate against Germany. This was counter-balanced by a sermon on the radio. Monty said to me "if you get fed up with this war you know what to do". Seriously though, I queried in my diary "Could I ever marry him?"
18th September	Out to cottage. Lobster salad for supper. Listened to the wireless. HMS Courageous had been sunk "But we got the U-Boat," Saw the film the 'Hound of the Baskervilles', Quite amusing.

Listened to vile German propaganda on the wireless.

22nd September	Philip arrived. He hadn't been called up yet. We went for a short walk in the rain, had tea at the Gaumont and saw Humphrey Bogart in 'King of the Underworld' at the Regal. To the Midland Hotel, where I had three sherries.

23rd September	Over to the cottage for lunch, then Philip left and I went for a long walk by myself through the wood and saw rabbits galore. A lovely evening. Listened to 'Bandwagon' and slept at the cottage.
24th September	Sunday. I fished in the evening. My father came over and we walked to the bridge. The stars were very clear and the moon bright.
25th September	First autumnal morning, sun and frost.
26th September	Washed my hair in Lux and vinegar. Read some of my old Birmingham diaries in bed. 'What a full life I've led so far. I hope I shall live to do something great. I am, as yet unfulfilled." I presume I meant as an actress.
29th September	Filled in National Registration Form
30th September	Went on a crowded train up to London, all agog to start the next stage of my training at RADA.

❧ VIII ❧
1940

LEARNING THE CRAFT. Julius Caesar in Modern Dress

2nd October

First day back. Only sixty students this term. Elizabeth and I had got a double remove to the top class. The girls in it were pretty awful. Quite a good timetable. I walked back to the digs across Regents Park with Elizabeth. In the evening went with Teddy to the Brasserie Universelle. Drank two sherries and three vodkas and didn't turn a hair. Teddy rather loving in the taxi back to the digs. Next day I went in the black-out to see him off, went back to the digs and had a long talk with fellow student Jasmine. We became great friends. She was really beautiful, with lovely legs.

4th October

A good rehearsal with Neil Porter. Elizabeth and I saw the film 'L'Heure de Jour'. "Maurice Chevalier has more personality than anyone I have ever seen on stage or screen." We looked at hats at Galeries Lafayette.

5th October

Windy day. Interesting mime class.

6th October

Henry Cass gave us a wonderful talk on 'Acting and Life'. "If you believe in your destiny, your star, nothing can stop you." This prompted an emotional entry in my diary that evening. "I love the academy, and life is, and can be, so wonderful. I hope to go on living and enjoying it." This uncertainty about the future in wartime London explains our 'Carpe Diem' attitude to life. "May I at least be allowed to know love." It is obvious from this remark that I was still fancy-free though I seem to have inspired plenty of love in my boyfriends.

7th October	Saw 'The Little Review' at The Little Theatre with David. It was a good show starring Cyril Ritchard, Hermione Baddeley and Joyce Grenfell. She sang 'Daisy's Going Out with Bert.' Tea in the Ladies' Drawing Room at the Royal Empire Club. "David wants to marry me."
9th October	I went and blued fourteen and sixpence on two new hats, one very glamorous with red roses aloft. "Life is very good. I hope it lasts."
10th October	I was cast as Venus in the Tudor Masque in Clifford Baxter's 'Rose Without A Thorn' which RADA was taking to Charterhouse School.
11th October	We had a good rehearsal of 'The Rose' with Neil Porter. Michael, the fool, asked what 'clyster pipes' were used for. The actor Stephen Haggard gave us a talk on 'Presentation and Producing Plays'. "He looked very haggard (oh dear!) under the eyes". My allowance was late again. I needed to borrow money the next day.
13th October	Cass was very depressing and told me that I should act in modern plays, comedy. Felt very down and wept in Regents Park. David took me out to dinner at Père Obère's. Wore my new hat.

16th October	The diary comment was "Life is so good, but Hitler is a d….nuisance." To Palladium with David and saw a slapstick show. "Bud Flanagan and Teddy Knox magnificent."
17th October	Went with RADA group to see J.M. Synge's 'The Playboy of the Western World' at the Duchess Theatre. Elspeth March was "A dream of beauty and grace as the Widow Quin". John Chandos was over-emotional in the name part. Went backstage to see Hugh Griffiths, ex RADA student.

One of the disadvantages of the double and treble casting of the women in order to give them all the experience of acting in Shakespeare was shown up by my entry on October the 18th - "I was furious today, because just as we got to my scene in Othello we switched over to one of the other Desdemonas." Went to the British Drama League Library and studied Tudor history, manners and fashion.

19th October	Prepared for the next day's class with the great god Cass.
20th October	We had a marvellous Othello rehearsal with Neil Porter, (The jealousy scene between Iago and the Moor). In the afternoon, Cass said that I had a feminine figure and must play young girls, "Happy and sensitive ones".
22nd October	Worked at Voice Production in the morning. Then went with Elizabeth to hear the tub-thumpers at Speaker's Corner.
23rd October	There was a telling comment in the diary about the living conditions in my digs. "The gas is lasting a long time". You had to put money in a slot machine for the supply.

25th October	Claude Gurney gave us a talk "All the old charm blast him". Listened to Romeo and Juliet on the wireless. Alec Guinness and Nova Pilbeam in the leads.
26th October	Rehearsal of The Tudor Masque, which I didn't enjoy.
27th October	Got to the end of Othello. In a later class with Cass that day he said that I needed the confidence to "feel it inside and to have the pluck to get it out." "I must".

Out to Streatham Theatre to see 'The Importance of Being Earnest' with a star cast, John Gielgud, Edith Evans, Peggy Ashcroft, Gwen Ffrangcon-Davis. "Gielgud brilliant. Especially in Act Two."

Saturday 28th	By the weekend I was in dire straits because my allowance hadn't come. Listened to 'Bandwagon' on the wireless.
29th October	Phoned Elizabeth to say that I didn't want to go out that afternoon. No money. Nothing to eat from lunch onwards but I had three cups of tea. The wireless was a boon.
30th/31st October	Two good rehearsals of 'Rose Without a Thorn'.
1st November	Othello rehearsal. Neil Porter liked my Desdemona. We had a good talk from Cass about jobs. He told us that we must make our own theatre and form our own companies. On the next day he continued with the subject and said that we must be 'people of the

theatre'. He told us that Gielgud was 'a man of the theatre'. Met my cousin Eleanor and we saw 'Bachelor Mother'. My non-politically correct comment was, "Ginger Rogers has a lovely figure but is common".

3rd November   In class Cass said that I needed a fresh attack but was "quite good". "Saw the film Mayerling. Superb, the whole mystery of love and death in it."

4th November   To see agents O'Brien, Linnit and Dunfee. Met Philip for a drink at the Cumberland. Then we had dinner at the Brasserie Universelle before going on to The Criterion to see 'The French for Love'. "Alice Delysia exquisite and good acting from Cecil Parker. A pity that Philip was so dull."

5th November   He and I went to hear the tub-thumpers at Hyde Park. Lunch at Stewart's. Then I listened to 'Henry V' on radio. Leslie was good as the King.

6th November   Had no lunch. Acted Cordelia in 'King Lear' in class.

8th November   Actor John Wyse gave us a talk. I noted "Very conceited and tight voice-production" but he was obviously tired. Later we had a good rehearsal of Othello with Neil Porter.

9th November   A good day's work. Masque in lunch hour. Alan Badel brought a book on Henry Irving round to me.

10th November   Felt frightfully depressed. Cass said that my acting was "very good for a schoolgirl" but my emotion didn't come through. I didn't feel it in my innermost being and that my work was good, clear, intelligent, but my mind was too much in evidence. He said that it would come and that I must practise very emotional material. On re-reading my diary I felt that he was giving me a tough time. But my reaction was increased determination. "I must let myself go. But I do need a love affair. I am so lonely." This was in spite of the attentions of my various boy friends, but I wasn't emotionally involved with any of them.

11th November

David and I saw J.B. Priestley's 'Music at Night' at the Westminster Theatre. "Robert Harris was charming." It was a tightly-constructed play until Act Three, where it fell apart.

Next we went to Odenino's, then to the Captain's Cabin then the Quality Inn and the Café Royal before going out to David's home at Claygate (where did we find the energy?). "A busy Sunday. Riding in the morning, skating at Richmond in the afternoon. David was very trying."

13th November

Back to London. We heard that some of us were to walk on in the crowd scenes in Henry Cass's modern dress production of Julius Caesar at the Embassy Theatre, Swiss Cottage. Listened in to Wendy Hiller in George Bernard Shaw's 'St Joan'. "She has vitality and sincerity, in contrast to the usual Kensington English actress."

15th November

Worked at "Rose". To Embassy for Julius Caesar rehearsal. I felt a bit lost but thought that it was going to be marvellous.

16th November

Voice production class "I must get my top notes smoother". JC rehearsal at The Embassy.

17th November	A lovely day. Rehearsed with Porter in the morning and with Cass in the afternoon. In the verse-speaking class I spoke 'White In the Moon the Long Road Lies' from A.E. Housman's 'A Shropshire Lad'. Dead silence when I'd finished. I'd held my audience. No tea. JC Rehearsal from three-thirty to seven.
18th November	Wonderful day. Elizabeth and I went to the Embassy Theatre for a JC rehearsal of four hours. Clifford Evans and Godfrey Kenton (who was most attractive) spoke to me "Life is wonderful."
20th November	Busy day. 'Rose' rehearsal then competitions. I won Mrs Lack's prize for diction, was highly commended in the Bossom and Dialect Competitions, and very highly marked in the Tree. JC rehearsal "I love them."
21st November	Dress rehearsal of 'Rose'. "My Venus is alright, I think." JC rehearsal. I believe that Clifford Evans (Cassius) rather likes me.
22nd	Second dress rehearsal of 'Rose' then JC rehearsal. Had chat with Clifford Evans.
23rd	Voice production class. JC rehearsal.
24th	Still no allowance from home. Othello rehearsal and later JC rehearsal on the stage. I listened to the quarrel scene between Brutus and Cassius. I thought that Mark Anthony,(Eric Portman) was "a bit queer."
25th	A five-hour JC rehearsal. Cassius winked at me. He was giving a very good performance. I can still remember the way he spoke his lines before the battle scene;

"Forever and forever, farewell, Brutus!
If we do meet again, we'll smile indeed;
If not, 'tis true this parting was well made."

Vivienne Bennett who was playing Portia was "not so frightfully good. I could do better." Obviously my confidence in my acting ability had survived the adverse criticism from Cass.

26th	Another marathon evening with David. After the tea-dance at Odenino's we went to Eros News Film followed by drinking at the Captain's Cabin, food at the Quality Inn and we finished the evening at the Café Royal.
27th	Final dress rehearsal of JC. Brutus and Cassius looked wonderful in their S.S. uniforms. Cass's chosen period was just before the Second World War during the dictatorships of Hitler and Mussolini.

The quarrel scene was marvellous. I loved being in the crowd scenes, especially the second one based on accounts of Jew-baiting in Germany.

3rd Plebian	"Tear him to pieces; he is a conspirator!"
Cinna	"I am Cinna the poet. I am Cinna the poet"
28th	To the Embassy for a long and trying second dress rehearsal. But I adored every minute of it. I thought that the production was going to be good. The stars were very nice to we students in that show. I had one line in the forum scene as the third Plebeian

"We'll hear him. Noble Anthony, go up"

Eric Portman said "When Laurie says that line I know that it's my turn to mount the rostrum."

At the last minute Cass suddenly had the idea of using a dug-out in the battle scene.

29th

After an Othello rehearsal, early to the Embassy for a terrible run-through. Eric Portman was very nervous in the forum scene and lost his temper. Clifford (Cassius) spoke to me. He was a Welsh Nationalist and was born in 1912 ("Is he married?").

First performance of JC at a matinee. It went well and the reviews were generally very good. "Praise to all the actors - and praise to the theatre for giving London its most powerful play, most modern play of the war" and "Mr. Cass's work has freshness, vigour, speed, invention" (Ivor Brown in the Observer). The most influential drama critic of the day, James Agate of the Sunday Times, wrote "Despite the modernisation and tom-foolery, the play the other night was highly effective and even moving. Mr Henry Cass, the producer, having called the tune, the actors at the Embassy pipe remarkably well."

The production was a novelty in London. It was long before the current habit emerged of updating a classic to make it 'relevant to the contemporary generation.'

20th

Rehearsed 'Rose' in the morning. The moves in the 'Masque' had been changed, and we had a difficult time with Liz Pizk our tutor. She was a brilliant teacher, but temperamental and I remember that she electrified us all at our first movement class by suddenly lifting up her long practice skirt and pulling it between her legs announcing "Now I em a man". She went on to write text books on movement.

Matinee of JC. Portman was still shaky on words. There were very few in the audience. Clifford Evans came down early in the interval and we had a chat. He found out that I was nineteen and had three sisters, one of them an identical twin. He was charming. I was so excited that I couldn't sleep until three a.m.

December 1st	First performance of Othello. The school secretary, Ms. Saunders, said that it was the best Shakespeare production that they had ever seen at the Academy. I acted well as Desdemona and, I think, looked nice. Alan MacNaughtan was wonderful as Othello. "And to think that he'll soon be called up."
December 2nd	Matinée of Julius Caesar. Clifford and I exchanged a few words, "Does he like me?"

After tea-time we heard that the show was going to transfer to His Majesty's Theatre after Christmas. There was a good house for the evening performance. Henry Cass said that Elizabeth and I acted well in the crowd scenes and would be missed when the production transferred. In the event we did go to His Majesty's.

After the interval Henry, Elizabeth and I watched the rest of the play. "The dug-out scene loses grip".

December 4th	Tea in my digs with Jasmine. We were a mutual admiration society. The war was getting me down, and I made a complete fool of myself on the 5th. I told Cass that I was depressed and cried with mascara running all over my face. He asked me if I'd been hurt and I told him about Teddy being at the Front. He and Jasmine were very comforting.
December 6th	Two shows.
December 7th	Morning rehearsal of 'The Rose'. Jasmine's people came to the JC matinee and we had tea in the club.
December 8th	Rehearsal of 'The Rose'. That evening Cassius said that they'd love me as Venus. "He is wonderful."

December 9th	On the Saturday we left by coach for Charterhouse. I sat next to Alan. The virginals, a pair of spinets which provided the music for 'The Masque', fell off the back of the coach. There was a cry of "There go the Virginals!" On arrival we were taken to our billets by Sir John Reith's cousin. At the dinner, following the performance, our Principal Sir Kenneth made a speech but I can't remember what he said.

December 9th

On the Saturday we left by coach for Charterhouse. I sat next to Alan. The virginals, a pair of spinets which provided the music for 'The Masque', fell off the back of the coach. There was a cry of "There go the Virginals!" On arrival we were taken to our billets by Sir John Reith's cousin. At the dinner, following the performance, our Principal Sir Kenneth made a speech but I can't remember what he said.

December 10th

We were shown around the school chapel. Then Tony and I motored to Osney Lodge for lunch. We listened to Lord Haw-Haw on the wireless in the evening. On the Sunday I walked five miles with Tony and the dogs. We went for a bike ride in the afternoon and heard Lord Haw-Haw again in the evening.

December 12th

Into the Academy. There was a party - great fun. Then to the Embassy. Cassius and I stood in the wings and he caressed me so much that I felt a little alarmed. "He is attractive."

December 13th

During the interval in the evening show he said "May I call you Rona?" Re-reading this all these years later I am amazed at the courtship etiquette of those days. "May I call you Rona?" indeed! And after all the embracing of the day before. Godfrey Kenton quoted from Romeo and Juliet to us.

December 14th

On my way to the theatre in the black-out I banged my head. Cassius was sympathetic and gave me brandy in his dressing-room and Eric Portman was solicitous.

| December 15th | Met George for lunch at the Cumberland Hotel. We had an early dinner at the Brasserie Universelle before the show. |

December 15th — Met George for lunch at the Cumberland Hotel. We had an early dinner at the Brasserie Universelle before the show.

December 16th — This was the last performance at the Embassy after a short run. We were to open at His Majesty's on December 23rd.

December 20th — First rehearsal at His Majesty's. There were now a lot of old men in the crowd.

December 21st — Everything went wrong. The actors made a fuss about their salaries. I gave Cassius a white, ivory elephant for luck which pleased him greatly. I am getting on well with Henry now, in a purely platonic way.

December 22nd — A five-hour rehearsal. I sat by Henry in the stalls and took notes on the lighting for him. He called me "the perfect secretary". Stayed working on the lighting with him and Jasmine until midnight.

December 23rd — Opening performance at the matinee. Cassius was very good and I told him so afterwards. He kissed my cheek and asked me to have coffee with him after the evening performance. I went and felt terribly disappointed because I felt that he wasn't keen on me. He didn't see me home. "Is he interested in Jasmine?" I was afraid so. "All right I'll d... well make him care for me!"

I spent that Christmas with Jasmine's family in Fareham. On Christmas Eve I travelled down to Portsmouth in a first-class carriage with Jasmine's mother (an Admiral's widow) and Jasmine's sister Delicia. Jasmine and I dozed all the way down. After lunch we decorated the tree.

Christmas Day	Church in the morning. After dinner Jasmine and I slept. There was another big meal in the evening.
Boxing Day	Jasmine and I returned to London. Taxi to theatre for the matinee.
27th December	Went to see an agent in the morning. Out with David between the shows.
December 28th	Cassius asked me out to tea. I sat between him and Godfrey and recited Andrew Marvell's poem 'To His Coy Mistress'

'Had we but world enough and time,
This coyness, Lady, were no crime.'

"Life is good".

December 29th	Cassius upset me by saying "Ships that pass in the night" and said that we would never see each other again. "Did he mean it?" I cried real tears in the forum scene. Felt awfully depressed because the notice went up. The show is going to end after a short run, to make way for a play featuring Sally Gray, the film-star made famous by 'Dangerous Moonlight'. Cassius asked me to his dressing-room at the end of the performance. He kissed me gently several times and said that I was "very, very sweet." I managed to save my face by telling him that if I'd met him two years earlier I would have been in love with him.
December 30th	Last performance. Cassius said he was sorry not to be seeing "his Rona" again. During the evening he asked Jasmine and me to go out with him afterwards. We went to his dressing-room. He obviously didn't want to be left

alone with me. Then we all went to the Café Royal and the talk was about a possible tour in Canada. I felt miserable because I believed he was fond of Jasmine. "I went home alone by bus". A pathetic entry.

December 31st   Awful crowded journey home to Derby. Everyone was appalled by how tired I looked. There was a party at home. George got rather tight and chased me up the back stairs to give me a kiss, quoting from Macbeth.

'That which hath made them drunk hath made me bold'

Sat up talking to my twin until four a.m.

So ended my first experience in a West End Theatre - and also my first romance. This time my feelings had been engaged. Although Julius Caesar had had only two short runs it had been a wonderful chance for we students, even if we were only in two crowd scenes. And to be acting at His Majesty's Theatre with all its great traditions was a privilege. Our big dressing-room was on the top floor and had direct access to the gallery through a connecting door. Once our two scenes were over by the interval, I often used to creep into the back row of the Gods and watch the rest of the play. To this day I know big chunks of it by heart and not only the most famous passage,

'Friends, Romans, Countrymen, lend me your ears.'

Godfrey Tearle who had replaced Eric Portman as Mark Anthony, had a beautiful voice and I can hear him now speaking his tribute to the murdered Caesar.

'O pardon me, thou bleeding piece of earth,
That I am meek and gentle with these butchers!'

He did not take kindly to the idea of Shakespeare in modern dress and I was amused to notice that in the battle-scenes he folded his great-coat round him like a toga.

Although some of the criticism that I had been given in class was quite strong, I felt that on the whole it had been justified and this had only strengthened my determination to improve my acting ability and of course the highlight of the year had been taking part in JC at His Majesty's. So 1939 ended with my fourth term at RADA and my first appearance on the West End stage.

TOURING. The English Classical Players

The year started well. I heard that I had won the Principal's Medal and my friend Alan had won the prestigious. Gold. In the spring I was touring with RADA's production of Twelfth Night. I found the part of Viola a joy. However tired I was, the beauty of Shakespeare's verse never failed to move me, especially in the scene with Orsino when Viola, disguised as his page Cesario describes the nature of love.

> 'Ay, but I know
> Too well what love women to men may owe.
> In faith, they are as true in heart as we.
> My father had a daughter lov'd a man
> As it might be perhaps, were I a woman,
> I should your Lordship.
> .... She never told her love
> But let concealment like a worm i' th' bud,
> Feed on her damask cheek. She pined in thought;
> And with a green and yellow melancholy
> She sat like Patience on a monument
> Smiling at grief.'

On April 1st we gave a performance at a school in Brighton. The children were restless and I didn't enjoy it. But we had managed to get digs for five shillings. Living expenses always had to be considered because of my small allowance

I was given a great deal of support by the Johnson family all the time that I was a student at RADA, in London rehearsing or having a break from touring. Dr. Johnson, a General Practitioner was an old friend of my father's. He had a practice at Streatham Hill and I used to play tennis there at weekends. And I was often asked, as a guest, to the Johnson's favourite hotel, the Pack Horse Inn, which was on the river at Staines. The Doctor had two sons, Ian and Derek (Dick). They were both medical students at St. Mary's Hospital, Paddington. Dick became one of my boyfriends. He was teased because he was always carting my heavy luggage to and from stations and my various digs. He proposed to me during an air-raid.

April 3rd	I went on a round of agents, met Philip for lunch and we saw a News film. The next day I had lunch with Henry Cass and met Griffith Jones "Very good looking but dumb" and saw Henry's production of Eugene O'Neill's 'Desire Under The Elms' at the Westminster Theatre and had tea with Robert Marsden. Back to digs. Teddy was home on leave and took me to The Cottage in Mayfair. He got very tight and proposed.
April 5th	Lunch with fellow student Jean Hardwicke. Then out with Teddy to the Renaissance Club. Afterwards we went to The Wellington, Café Royal and Savoy Grill. Jack Hulbert, Cicely Courtneidge and Marie Tempest were all there. Back to digs at one-thirty a.m.
6th April	Saturday. Home to Derby
8th April	Teddy came over for coffee. He was drinking too much and worried me.
9th April	We heard that Hitler had invaded Norway.
10th April	"My sisters are getting me down."
11th April	A desperate entry. "I must get away from home." But my parents were being considerate.

13th April	A wire arrived from my agent Miriam Warner telling me I had to go up to London on the next Monday about a job. "Thank the Lord, at last!"
14th April	A lovely sunny windy day. Went out to the cottage and fished a bit, using a worm, but no good.
15th April	Up to town. To digs. Lunch at Lyons corner house. Then to the Players Club for the interview. I was told that I had a ninety per cent chance of getting the job.
16th April	Teddy and I saw the film 'Pinocchio'. Then he took me to the Criterion and out to the Renaissance Club. Back to Derby. No news at home about the interview.
17th April	I was in town having a coffee at Boots when Mimi phoned to say I'd got the job. Joy all round.
21st April	Saw the film 'Escape To Happiness' featuring a lovely girl Ingrid Bergman, "she is the part", and Leslie Howard.
22nd April	I went to the first rehearsal of 'As You Like It' in St Martin's Lane. The company was called the English Classical Players. It toured schools with a repertoire of three plays performed mainly out of doors. That year it was in its twenty-sixth tour. The chosen plays were 'As You Like It' 'The Tempest' and George Bernard Shaw's 'You Never Can Tell.' We travelled in our own bus. Our wardrobe and props went with us at the back. When we arrived at our venues we had to set up the minimal staging. After the performance we had to strike the set and reload it and also pack

our costumes and props in the bus. Our schedule was so crowded that we sometimes arrived at one of our out of doors venues too late to plan and rehearse the exits and entrances. On one occasion during the performance of 'As You Like It' this caused some embarrassment. As the banished Celia accompanied by Rosalind and Touchstone were fleeing along a path having been banished by the Duke, to their horror they saw him and his followers coming towards them on the same path. All they could do was to brush past them with averted faces, pretending they couldn't see them. Otherwise the plot would have been wrecked.

Because of the call-up of young actors, the company was a mixture of elderly and old ones and young people, like myself, straight out of drama school. Compromises in the casting were therefore inevitable. In 'The Tempest' I was given the unlikely double of Iris, Goddess of the Rainbow and Trinculo, a drunken jester. This meant that I had to wear Iris's diaphanous robes underneath Trinculo's jester costume. I had to do a quick change in the wings or, more often, behind a bush, tearing off Trinculo's outfit to reveal Iris's floating draperies underneath. This spectacle amused the cast very much at first but they soon got used to it.

I was cast as Celia in 'As You Like It'. The Orlando was Alfred Burke who had a successful acting career afterwards. Monica Stutfield (a bishop's daughter) played Rosalind and the small part of Oliver was given to Richard O'Donoghue who subsequently went into theatre management and became a life long friend; Phyllis Liddell played Phoebe and Bryan Matheson Le Beau. Bryan is still working, a resident in Denville Hall, and playing character parts in television.

At the first reading of 'As You Like It' my diary entry was "I think I'm better than Rosalind." She has experience and is getting three pounds a week. "Whatever was I getting?" I was apparently full of confidence and conceit.

24th April	Letter from Root. He said that I was too interested in my acting, and not enough in him. "Too right about the latter".
26th April	I enjoyed the Tempest rehearsals enormously. "I'll act in Shakespeare at the Old Vic one day." I never did.
30th April	My allowance was late again. "Money is a curse when you haven't any. And ten shillings doesn't go far."
3rd May	A wire from Root. Said he was coming down on leave. "Oh God!"
5th May	The tour had started.
17th May	A message from Root to say he had gone to France.
21st May	Heard from home that my twin's husband Tinny, who had gone to France with the Sherwood Foresters, was missing in action. Believed to have been captured by the Japanese, a terrible thought.
22nd May	We took the three plays around the country until the end of May giving performances, generally out of doors, to public schools and state junior and secondary ones. Among the places we visited were Chester where we walked along the walls, York, Lincoln, Lichfield where we saw over Dr. Samuel Johnson's house, Salisbury, when we were shown around the Cathedral, Bristol and Leeds. It was there on May 31st we sat up and watched the troops who had been evacuated from Dunkirk marching from the

station, tired but cheeky, singing 'Tipperary'. Air raids were expected and the children had to be evacuated. Signposts were being taken down from the roads.

We couldn't find any digs in Bristol, so we all had to sleep in the bus which was parked in the cattle market. Trains were shunted up and down all night. It was very cold for June. One member of the cast seized a heavy cloak from the back of the bus and used it as a blanket. The rest of us followed suit. I can't remember who the unfortunate person was who was left with Iris's flimsy costume.

I had run into a problem at the start of the tour. When I was playing Trinculo in the Tempest. In the scene when I took refuge from a coming storm under Caliban's gabardine he (Victor Woolf) who was sexually promiscuous seized the opportunity to fondle me. The audience might have thought that the wriggling and faint cries of protest were part of the plot.

Throughout the tour the war was never far away from our thoughts. Our programmes carried the notice "AIR RAID INSTRUCTION Please keep- calm and do not hurry unduly. There will be plenty of time to reach adequate shelter". I was more interested in how I was described in the cast list. I appeared twice as TRINCOLO (sic) A Jester, R. Laurie and as Iris, The Goddess of the Rainbow, Rona Laurie. That month Churchill addressed the House of Commons in a great speech "You ask what is our aim? I can answer in one word, it is victory, victory at all costs, victory in spite of terror; victory however long and hard the road may be."

31st May   I read in the papers that Root had been decorated with a DFC (Distinguished Flying Cross). Later he got a bar to it.

At the end of May I recorded *"War news is very bad. We'll have to evacuate France."*

3rd June   "Slept badly. Bombers overhead."

15th June   Monica and I dashed up to town and got stools at the Aldwych Theatre for 'The

Tempest'. Gielgud disappointed as Prospero, Jack Hawkins was excellent as Caliban, Miranda was relaxed and graceful but her voice was poor. Ariel had his moments. I met the actor John McCallum afterwards.

17th June — Heard that France had surrendered to Germany. We felt stunned. "Nazism here? Will we ask for peace? What will happen to our troops in France? Everyone thinks that we can't loose."

On the 19th we were in Salisbury. There was an air-raid warning at one-thirty a.m. We went down to the basement of our digs. I amused the others by looking at myself in a hand-mirror and saying "Well I'm glad to see that I'm still looking quite pink and cheerful."

24th & 25th June — Air-raids. But I managed to sleep through most of them.

26th June — End of tour. Back to town. Farewell drinks at the Prince Albert Pub.

This tour had been a valuable experience. There had been the challenge of playing out of doors and on different school stages. Despite the long journeys and the exhausting days sometimes with two shows following a rehearsal in the morning, and the constant difficulty of finding digs, the enthusiasm in the company and the good-fellowship had made my first experience of a professional tour enjoyable and worthwhile.

Photo of Rona Laurie by Angus McBean

∞X∞
1940

RESTING. An Interlude and Change of Direction

27th June

Looking for a job. Round nine agents but only managed to see two. Root phoned and we went to Lansdowne House. He told me all about his war-time experiences. He is desperately anxious for me to marry him. He brought me back to my digs and we had a long talk on the doorstep, much to the annoyance of my landlord. I was very upset and didn't sleep well.

28th June

Saw agents Jim Moran and Haddon Mason. Lunch at the Lantern with Bryan and Phyllis. Out to Croydon to see Root. On the Saturday Jasmine popped in and we had a good talk. She thought it would be a good idea to have a provisional engagement. To Renaissance Club with Dicky O'Donoghue. He was very shocked about Root and said how bored I would be as an RAF wife. Michael Redgrave was there. Bed at two-thirty a.m.

30th June

Sunday. Met Root in Regents Park and told him that I couldn't give up my career for him. He was very shaken and so was I, but I knew that I had made the right decision. Thank God I'd been given the strength to say 'no' to him.

"What am I to do now? I must get work. Allowance late."

2nd July — A blitz was expected today. Letter from Root. He was utterly miserable. "God, I wish I loved him a little more or a little less."

3rd July — Saw 'Gone With The Wind'. Clark Gable, Vivien Leigh, Leslie Howard and Olivia de Havilland, all excellent and ideally cast. A faithful portrayal of the novel.

4th July — Saw some agents today. Lunch at the Lantern with Dicky. He whisked me off to see 'New Faces' again. To Rules afterwards. "If only Dicky and Root could be combined. Each has what the other lacks."

5th July — Saw some agents including Mrs. Nelson King. Went to matinee of a charity show 'All Clear' at the Globe. Bea Lillie wonderful. Noel Coward spoke at the interval. Gielgud appeared in a Chekhov sketch. "I am not so blind about him as I was". Saw manager Harry Hanson and didn't impress him, though dressed in my best.

8th July — Saw Rodney Millington at 'Spotlight'. Lunch at Queens Hotel with Dicky and then home to Derby. My sisters were being difficult.

9th July — Jim, my father's ex-batman and now an odd-jobs man for the family, drove me out to Dove Cottage.

10th July — Fished abortively in the morning. We continued to shoot down enemy raiders. If only I could get a job soon. Mimi and Pauline were both rather cruel to me. "I will succeed."

13th July	The war seemed distant despite the noise of planes, searchlights and the smell of the smokescreen.
14th July	Listened into 'Twelfth Night'. Churchill made a speech "Invasion may come this night, next week, never."
15th July	There was an earth tremor at twelve p.m., we spent half the night in the cellar. It was a bomb. I was busy with black-out curtains to satisfy air-raid precautions.
16th July	Saw propaganda film 'Careless Talk Costs Lives'.
25th July	Went up to London and made an appointment for the next day to have my photo taken by Angus McBean, the most celebrated theatrical photographer of the day. His subjects included John Gielgud and Vivien Leigh.
26th July	To Angus McBean's studio. Had great fun. We chatted for an hour. Out to Renaissance Club. Henry Savage gave a talk and Michel Redgrave and Hugh Miller were there. I think it was at this club that I first met Jack Bartlett. He was an RAF pilot and often took me to the Brevet and Aero Clubs when he was on leave in London.
27th July	Saw agent Haddon Mason. Met Dick Johnson and went with him to the film 'Rebecca'. It was very good, particularly George Sanders as Favell and Joan Fontaine as Mrs. de Winter.
29th July	Met Jack at the Aero Club. Then we had drinks at The Mayfair.

30th July	Went to Hatchett's. "He dances so well and is a comfort to me." During the month that I spent at home I went out to Dove Cottage several times before returning to London.

The main phase of the Battle of Britain started on August 8th. Of course we didn't know that at the time.

14th August	Air raid.
16th August	I noted, "RAF are doing wonderfully".
19th August	A big air-raid.
25th August	Planes came over in the night. We were in the cellar and heard the bombs dropping.
27th August	Two lots of sirens.
31st August	Air-raid.
28th September	Five air-raids.
14th October	Air-raid.
20th October	Air-raid warning.
27th October	Air-raid. Slept badly. Dreamt that I was being machine-gunned by the Nazis.
1st August	To see 'Till the Day I Die' with Bryan. It was well acted.
2nd August	Met Jasmine and we journeyed down to Portsmouth.
3rd August	Breakfast on the terrace. A lovely house.
4th August	We all played tennis. There had been two air-raids the evening before but on the 4th we had a night of quiet sleep. To morning church.
5th August	Two air-raids. We saw the anti-aircraft fire.
6th August	Long, dull journey to Devizes to stay with Pamela at Urchfont Vicarage.

9th August	To Tank Corps dinner at Bullerton Camp. Met Major Rodney Martin, who never left me all evening. (Pamela said he was married).
10th August	Had tea with Rodney in the Bear Hotel in Devizes and stayed on talking. I caught the seven-thirty train back to London arriving at ten-thirty p.m.
11th August	Train to Derby. Listened in to 'Johnson over Jordan'. Ralph Richardson very good.
12th August	Leaflets were dropped.
15th August	Heard that Croydon Airport had been bombed. Was worried about Root.
19th August	A big raid. Bombs fell near our house and hit the Derby High School gates just down the road.
25th August	My photos arrived from Angus McBean. They were very good indeed. My father paid for them. "Whoopee!" Planes came over in the night. We were in the cellar and heard the bombs dropping. The Rolls Royce Factory was obviously one of the targets. Its roof had been camouflaged as a village green complete with duck-pond, but as far as I can remember it never got a direct hit.
27th August	My father asked me if I would like to stay at the Green Man Hotel in Ashbourne. I was thrilled. Jim ran me up there.
17th September	Mimi told me that Root was married. I felt awful but disguised it pretty well I thought. However, it was the cause of a good deal of heart-burning on my part.
28th September	The officers of an Indian Regiment were billeted in the hotel. Their commanding officer was Colonel Hill and I had dinner

with him and Major Ginger Apcar that first
evening. Ginger told me later that it was love
at first sight and all through September and
half of October he courted me, taking me out
to lunch, tea and dinner and over to
Nottingham several times. He proposed to me
more than once and gave me expensive
presents, rings and a regimental brooch of
diamonds and sapphires which Mimi and
I agreed, rather reluctantly, would have to be
sent back. Jack Bartlett was stationed at
Matlock and I sometimes went over to play
golf with him. It was an uneasy relationship.
We were both nervous with each other. He
didn't propose. Mimi described him as a
'London' type. I don't think that she meant it
as a compliment.

I was out of work from the end of June when the English
Classical Players tour finished, living at home during August and
September, apart from a brief visit to Wiltshire and a short stay at
the Green Man hotel. Ginger's courtship and the rounds of golf
I played with Jack took my mind off the war despite the bombing
and Dove Cottage was a wonderful refuge. The nights I spent there
were genuinely peaceful and I enjoyed the fly-fishing although
I was not markedly successful at catching trout.

In mid-October my agent told me that I had been offered a job
as head of the newly established Drama Department at the Arts
Educational School. This was a well-known ballet school run jointly
by the three Cone sisters, Miss Gracie, Miss Valli and Miss Lily,
and Mrs Olive Ripman. It had just been evacuated from London to
Loddington Hall, Lord Allerton's country seat. The house had
hardly been lived in. As I was out of work I accepted the post. This
prompted an outburst from Mimi and a lecture on marriage. She
said that I wouldn't let myself fall in love because of my career.

On the 21st October Churchill broadcast a speech to the Free French. It contained the laconic remark "We are waiting for the long-promised invasion. So are the fishes."

On the 9th November I drove through lovely scenery to Loddington Hall and was welcomed by two of the Miss Cones. I started teaching on the 11th and loved it but felt completely exhausted at the end of the day.

13th November	I gave some one to one lessons.
14th November	A moonlight night. A number of planes came over - there was a raid somewhere in the Midlands. Slept badly.
15th November	Took the babies' class. Material used was 'The King's Breakfast' by A.A. Milne. David, calling himself my cousin, called and took me into Leicester where we had dinner at the Stag and Pheasant.
16th November	Off with David to play golf. Then into Leicester to see the Regency Players' Production of George Bernard Shaw's 'The Devil's Disciple' starring Robert Donat. He gave a good performance but spoiled it by a conceited curtain speech. We danced at the Palais. David proposed again. Two bombs fell near Loddington during the night.
18th November	A good day's work. The Principals came down after a ghastly night in London. I discussed my pupils with Miss Gracie.
19th November	Black-outs were being put up.
20th November	I moved from the Hall to the stable. Worked at timetables till late-ish. Awful night with landmines and bombs. Didn't sleep till four a.m.

21st November	Walked by the lake. Lovely Rackham (a famous illustrator) country.
22nd November	A hectic day. All Principals here. Worked at timetable till late. Miss Gracie had suddenly altered her whole idea about the drama course. Letter from Hanz Lederer.
23rd November	Home to Derby. Pauline met me with Jim. Mimi seemed very depressed.
25th November	Back to Loddington. Took mime class. Letter from Jack "He is a comfort". Lord Allerton called. "Very attractive with fair hair."
26th November	Dining room duty. I got on well with the children. Took senior mime class and started another class for reading aloud. I used Kenneth Graham's 'The Wind in The Willows' as material.
27th November	Took a good intermediate drama class. Had a lovely letter from Jack.
28th November	Gunfire during the night.
30th November	Duty weekend.
1st December	Sunday. Party over at the stables - a great success. The staff were well away on two or three sherries.
2nd December	A good junior mime class. Walked up to the pub in the evening. A moonlit Arthur Rackham scene, owls hooting. It reminded me of Wordsworth's Prelude.
3rd December	Took mime class in front of Miss Lily and Miss Valli. They said that it was excellent. Duty in dining room.
4th December	A photographer from the Daily Mirror came and took photos all day. Two of my mime

class, others by the lake and in the staff-room. We drank sherry on the Daily Mirror.

7th December — Into Leicester by school bus to stay with old friends. Saw the bomb damage; devastated houses and a bit of a landmine in a tree.

10th December — Enjoyed 'A Midsummer Night's Dream' rehearsal with the Mendelssohn music but felt that it was all a bit end-of-termish.

13th December — The Principals arrived. A performance to the rest of the school of 'A Midsummer Night's Dream' and 'The King's Breakfast'. It went very well. Miss Gracie and Miss Lily were charming about it and the girls cheered me. I was quite overcome and too excited to sleep.

14th December — Performance of 'The Dream' to mostly local yokels.

15th December — Carol service in church.

16th December — A moonlit night. Searchlights.

17th December — Lord Allerton arrived in riding kit.

20th December — Home to Derby. Air-raid. Slept in cellar.

22nd December — Philip arrived and took me out to lunch.

23rd December — Air-raid.

25th December — Christmas day.

29th December — I looked forward to starting my second term at Loddington. I had more confidence as a teacher but regarded the job as only temporary and my determination to have a stage career was as strong as ever.

1940 had been an eventful year and I had enjoyed two tours, one with RADA and the other with the English Classical Players.

My 'resting' period ended with the engagement as a drama tutor at the Arts Education School. I knew this would soon end and I was staying optimistic about my future in the theatre in 1941.

THE TRAVELLING THEATRE AND WEEKLY REPERTORY. Ordeal By Fire

I continued running the new Drama Department at the school for two more terms. Two of my students became famous in the world of ballet. John Gilpin, a gifted young dancer and Gillian Pyrke who subsequently changed her name to Gillian Lynne. She achieved a worldwide reputation as a choreographer following her brilliant work in Andrew Lloyd Webber's musical 'Cats'. At Loddington she had shown promise as a dancer and actress. At the time I first knew her she had just lost her mother. As it happened the Regency Players Repertory Company in Leicester were going to produce Dodie Smith's 'Dear Octopus' and the Cones were asked if they would allow one of their pupils to play the part of Scrap, whose mother had just died. At first, the Principals were hesitant about putting Gill forward as they felt that she might be upset by the coincidence, however, they eventually thought that the experience might help her to get through this difficult time. Her father, Major Pyrke, agreed and she herself certainly wanted to play the part. It was necessary for her to have a chaperone and the Cones suggested me. The part of Laurel had not yet been cast and it was proposed that I should fulfil both jobs. Gill and I both enjoyed our week at the Theatre Royal.

After the third term at the school, I decided that it was time to move on. At the end of 1941 Spotlight got me a job with a touring company, The Travelling Theatre, run by Felicity (Fay) Douglas, the actress and playwright. The headquarters were at Wash Common, just outside Newbury. We took a repertoire of plays to Army, Navy and Air force stations in Berkshire, Hampshire and

Wiltshire. Our venues ranged from town halls, guildhalls, corn exchanges to tents. Among the places we visited were Portsmouth, Andover, Swindon and Worthy Down. As with the English Classical Players, we carried our costumes and props in our bus, while the minimal scenery was transported by our van. We had to set up and dismantle the set for each performance. It was an unsubsidised company and run on a shoe-string, using young actors and actresses. I was engaged originally to stage-manage and play small parts. However, on arrival I was immediately cast as the juvenile lead, and while continuing to stage-manage, I generally played that part throughout the tour. I hadn't kept a diary during this period. I expect because I was working too hard, but I have all the programmes. Some reflect war-time conditions "Owing to the paper shortage and in answer to the Government appeal, we are using old programmes GOD SAVE THE KING."

When Frank Vosper's 'Love from a Stranger' was produced I was cast as Ethel the Maid and Fay's son Toby played the boot boy. He became a well-known director, running the Prospect Theatre based in Mold in North Wales. Three incidents stand out in my memory of that tour. The first was when we were near the Fleet Air Arm station at Worthy Down. During the performance, the door began to shake (our scenery was always rickety). An officer had come backstage. Fay issued a peremptory order to him, "Hold that door firm". He meekly obeyed. It was Laurence Olivier who had enlisted for war-time service. The second incident was the occasion when we were playing in a tent at Shrivenham. During a performance an oil-lamp on the stage caught fire. A burly sergeant sitting in the front row dashed onto the stage, seized the lamp and flung it outside. The third episode was during War Ship week in Portsmouth. That late December we were performing at the Guildhall. When we couldn't get back to our base in Wash Common after a show we were given hospitality. This varied from the lavish (rarely) to the frugal (quite often). Some of our hosts didn't seem to realise how hungry we were after travelling to the venue, setting up the scenery, giving a performance and then packing everything up afterwards. There was rarely any time to eat. That particular night Fay and I were billeted in the Admiral's house. We arrived there very late, exhausted and ravenous. No food was offered. My room was in an attic, obviously a maid's bedroom. It was perishingly cold. I was reduced to putting the threadbare piece of carpet on top of the bed-clothes. In the small hours of the morning the door creaked open and I heard Fay's whisper, urging me to come down with her to raid the larder. When I hesitated she said, "I am your Director, Rona. And I order you to obey me." We crept down to the kitchen, opened the fridge door and gobbled up some leftovers. We left the next morning undetected.

Looking back on that tour I can hardly believe how hard we had to work. Here is a typical two-day schedule drawn up by Fay for the company:

MONDAY

	Costumes fetched by car.
7.00p.m.	Dress rehearsal at Woodhay with lighting and hand-props.
	Get there and back under your own steam
	Give Performance

TUESDAY

9:00 a.m.	Load Van
9:30 a.m.	Van arrives at Newbury Corn Exchange Take own suitcases down.
12:30 p.m.	Lunch
3:00 p.m.	Matinee
7:00 p.m.	Evening performance. Pack up everything ready for leaving next morning.

During this time I was able to get up to London once or twice to see agents and shows. I had an interview with Donald Wolfit at the Strand Theatre. He told me that I had good voice production and speech. That same day I managed to see two acts of the ballet Swan Lake at Sadler's Wells Theatre. Margot Fonteyn and Robert Helpmann were the principal dancers.

On the 26th January while I was still with the Travelling Theatre a letter arrived asking me to go up to Spotlight for an interview with Norman Buckle, whom I'd worked with on the English Classical Player tour. He was now Director of a repertory company based in the Castle Theatre, Farnham. I heard that I was accepted and on the 29th I said goodbye to the Travelling Theatre and departed to join the repertory company.

It was small and, just as with the English Classical Players, the casting was not to type. My repertoire of roles was certainly extended during the eight months that I was there. One week I was playing a seventy year old in Strindberg's 'Easter' and the next a sixteen year old adenoidal school girl in Noel Coward's 'Fumed Oak'. In between there were a few middle-aged parts. At that time I considered fifty to be very old indeed and I played these characters as if they were ninety, with a shaking voice and arthritic movements. The company could not afford to hire wigs so I used to sprinkle my hair with white talcum powder. Unfortunately, if anyone brushed against me or tapped me on the shoulder a cloud of white dust was released and if I went out in the rain it looked as if I had a bowl of porridge on my head. When I was playing a fifty year old in J. B. Priestley's 'Laburnum Grove' I happened to drop a pencil. As I bent creakily down to pick it up there was some laughter from the audience who were used to seeing me in young parts. Once, when I was playing an old lady I made an entrance which caused the cast to collapse with laughter. There was an old-fashioned stove in the wings. When we were waiting for our cue to go on we would stand by it learning the lines for next week's play. On this occasion the cast heard a loud slap which was my script being slammed down onto the stove, then scampering feet as I made for my entrance and then the door opened and the oldest woman in creation tottered onto the stage. Everyone nearly collapsed and I couldn't understand what was wrong with them.

When I describe the rehearsal schedule in the weekly repertory of those days my students can hardly believe it. They are used to a three week period of rehearsal, or more often six weeks and we had to rehearse the following week's play while appearing in eight performances of the current one. This was the timetable at Farnham and at most other weekly repertories in the country at that time.

MONDAY	Dress rehearsal and opening night of the week's play
TUESDAY	Rehearsal of Act 1 of next week's play. Evening Performance.
WEDNESDAY	Rehearsal of Act 2, Matinee and evening performance.
THURSDAY	Rehearsal of Act 3. Evening performance.
FRIDAY	Run through of Acts 1,2 & 3. Evening performance.
SATURDAY	Matinee and evening performance.
SUNDAY	Assemble one's costume and finish learning lines.

I was thought to be a 'quick-study' but by the time I had left my learning process had slowed down considerably because of the weekly pressure. We had to get through the first nights as best we could. Norman, our Director, was also our leading man and was always very shaky on his lines. I remember that once he had to read the third act. On Mondays the entire resources of prompter and cast were needed to get him through. It was a question of sink or swim for everyone and certainly moulded us into a team. The stage was small and the dressing room was immediately behind the back curtain. It was shared by men and women and was divided by a flimsy sheet stretched across the middle of the room and suspended by a string. One had to whisper during a performance in order not to be heard on the stage or in the auditorium. This was my first, and only, engagement in weekly repertory and could have been described as an ordeal by fire but the experience had the advantage of equipping one with the ability to cope ever after with a variety of domestic emergencies and I often tell my students today "If you can cope with weekly rep you can cope with anything."

Now I was working with more experienced actors and actresses who could handle their stage properties and at the same time speak their lines fluently while dealing with complicated stage business. At an early rehearsal I couldn't even manage to pour out a cup of tea without slowing down the action. The director watched me, at first with ill-concealed impatience and then with weary resignation. "Didn't they teach you <u>anything</u> at RADA?" However, I gradually managed to relax and ended by actually enjoying using properties. At least it was something to do with the hands - always a problem for young performers. During the first productions at Farnham, the pace was too fast for me. I felt like Alice in 'Through the Looking Glass' "And still the Queen kept crying, "Faster!" but Alice felt that she couldn't go any faster."

The day after I arrived we started rehearsing A.A. Milne's 'The Dover Road' and I saw the evening performance of Sutton Vane's 'Outward Bound'. Afterwards we danced on the stage and I met the leading lady of the company Evelyn Neilson. She had been a child actress at the Old Vic and became a life-long friend. Some years later I married her brother Edward. Evelyn always had great faith in my acting ability and it was she who advised me to leave repertory and try for something more ambitious.

In February I was cast as Stella in J.B. Priestley's 'Eden End'. This was my favourite part in the season and called for strongly emotional acting. During the rehearsals I managed to move some of the cast to tears. I remember that after my final exit at a late rehearsal I had a nerve-storm and couldn't stop crying. Having been criticised so often at RADA for not being able to release my feelings I felt that, at last, my training was beginning to bear fruit. However, I still had much to learn, not only about acting, but how to cope with technical difficulties caused by make-shift properties and insecure scenery. When I was playing a secretary in John van Druten's 'London Wall' I burst through the door into the office, forcing it open the wrong way <u>twice</u>.

After playing a series of young characters I was relieved to be told that I could have a week out in the following production. This was to be Anthony Armstrong's 'Ten Minute Alibi'. But my relief was short-lived. I was told that I had to sit on a high stool behind the set, draped in a black cloak and that my job was to move the minute hands of a clock which was hung on the back of the curtains in front of me. The whole plot hinged on the time that the clock registered. One night owing to a misunderstanding between the actor playing the murderer and me there was a struggle as we tried to move the hands in opposite directions. That night, the mystified audience saw a performance of 'Twenty Minute Alibi'. This, of course, had made nonsense of the plot. As I had been reluctant to lose my week out the director had graciously allowed my name to appear in the programme thus:

Not Appearing
MISS TICK TOCK - Rona Laurie

One advantage of Farnham was its nearness to London. One could go up and down in a day in order to see films and matinees of plays and also make a round of agents. I see from my diary that on 13th April I saw the film 'Dangerous Moonlight', was impressed by Anton Walbrook, the beauty of Sally Gray and the specially composed music by Richard Addinsell "the Warsaw Concerto". I saw Walbrook again on stage at the Aldwych in Lillian Hellman's 'Watch on the Rhine'.

Despite the punishing schedule of weekly repertory we were still able to enjoy a lively social life. We had a party after every opening night and were sometimes entertained by Mrs Rupert Anderson, a supporter of the Castle Theatre. She lived at Waverley Abbey, nearby. She had been a great friend of J.M. Barrie. Drinks were very cheap by today's standards and I noted "Cigarettes are nearly one penny and a quarter EACH". I gave up smoking for seven weeks. Because we were working so hard the war seemed remote, although I did some fire watching and worked in a Red Cross second hand shop.

The season ended on 11th July. It had been a useful experience, although at times a traumatic one. A wide range of plays had been produced; the playwrights included George Bernard Shaw, J.M. Barrie, J.B. Priestley, Strindberg, Somerset Maugham, Oscar Wilde, Thornton Wilder, Noel Coward and Terence Rattigan, but alas, no Shakespeare or Restoration comedy.

On 13th July I travelled back to London and visited the office of Spotlight, the casting directory. On the next day I went on a tour of the agents and again on the 17th, before I had a welcome break - four nights in Wiltshire with my school friend Pamela. I was dead tired. I suppose it was partly the reaction to leaving Farnham and partly the frustration of an unsuccessful round of agents.

21st July   Back to town. I tried to see the agents Elsie Beyer and Dorothy Black at H.M. Tennent's.

23rd July   I called on agents until I was blue in the face before going home to Derby.

There were air raids in Derby on the 24th and the 27th July. On the day after I went up to London with my parents and twin. The next day my father was decorated with a military C.B.E. at Buckingham Palace. Mimi and Joan went in with him and I waited outside. When he came out he joined me and we celebrated together in a nearby pub.

30th July   Derby had another air raid and we spent the night in the cellar. I noted that I felt too tired to worry about jobs, or, indeed anything. But I had at last acquired a London agent, Miriam Warner. Out of the blue a postcard arrived from her to say that Ralph Lynn was holding auditions to cast a play which he was taking out on tour. This was the Ben Travers' farce 'Thark'. It was one of the famous Aldwych farces first produced in 1927.

It was my first important audition and I didn't know what to expect. When I got to the theatre I was somewhat daunted to find that the auditorium was filled with young actresses all after the same part that I was, the ingénue played by Winifred Shotter in the original production. They looked so sophisticated. Some wore hats and I felt sure that they had had a lot of experience. Just before it was my turn to go up on the stage to sight-read the script, one of my rivals told me that she had heard that the part was already cast. This may have been designed to put me off, but it didn't and I went up on the stage not feeling nervous surprisingly enough. After reading for a few minutes I was stopped and called down into the stalls where Ralph Lynn and the tour manager were sitting and they told me that I had got the part. I realise now that one of the reasons I had been chosen was because Lynn was looking for an unsophisticated young girl. My simple primrose coloured cotton summer frock was in contrast to everyone else's smart outfit and I had always been a good sight-reader, having won prizes at school. I was so excited that I could hardly speak and I felt sure that they must have noticed my heart hammering against my ribs. I telephoned my surprised agent and she told me that I could call round at her office that afternoon and get my contract. I sent a telegram home "Ralph Lynn's leading lady arriving tonight."

I had already served eleven years' apprenticeship with touring companies and eight months in repertory. Now I was engaged to play a leading part with a first-class company, visiting some of the major cities in the provinces. I could hardly wait to begin rehearsing.

FINDING MY FEET. Touring In Thark

We started rehearsing 'Thark' on 20th August and we opened at the Pavilion Theatre, Torquay on 7th September. The dress rehearsal didn't go well, but the evening performance was much better and we got good notices in the local paper. "Ralph Lynn leads an excellent cast - a talented company" and "Rona Laurie is a charming and spirited heroine." I noted that air raids were affecting our business that week. On the Sunday we travelled to Reading for our next date. The company always had a reserved coach on the train and we shared picnic baskets. I was spoiled as I always had a seat in the principal's compartment. On that journey we had cold chicken.

It was at Reading that I was given some wise advice about how to handle my salary, which was six pounds a week. On the first pay day I was rushing off to spend the two pounds left over after I had paid the four pounds hotel bill, when a member of the company said "Oh no you don't. You go straight to the Post Office and open an investment account. Put a pound in every week and at the end of the tour you will have saved something to help you tide over the out of work period before your next job." I dutifully followed this advice and have always been grateful for it.

At that time touring was regarded in the profession as second-rate employment, in contrast to working in the West End. There was rather a cruel joke going around "Question: what is the difference between Laurence Olivier and Donald Wolfit? (He was a famous actor-manager) Answer: Olivier is a Tour de Force and Wolfit is a Force de Tour." However, I thoroughly enjoyed the experience. Even the Sunday travelling under wartime conditions, in unheated trains frequently arriving late after long delays. We often had to change at Crewe, well known as the Sunday meeting place of "actors and fish".

Having to search for lodgings in a strange town, late on a Sunday night was often a nightmare. But theatrical digs were cheap and sometimes hotels would give us a cut-rate. During rehearsals addresses were privately exchanged. I learned the hard way that it was a mistake to arrange to share digs every week with a newly-met member of the cast. You could be landed with an uncongenial companion for weeks on end. Some landladies were famous, their addresses a closely guarded secret only given to your friends. There were a few very good ones in Glasgow's Sauchiehall Street and you were lucky if you managed to book in with one of them. I was amused to read John Osborne's description of his touring experience, "Fifteen shillings a week might get you bed and breakfast in a place like Glasgow, but you might find yourself enacting the old gag of leaning against the wall in your overcoat to feel the warmth from the fire in the house next door." But there was nothing more comforting than to come back to your digs after the evening's performance to find a blazing coal fire in your bed sitter and a table laid for supper in front of it. If asked, landladies would do the catering for you for all your meals for an all-in charge of two pounds fifty for board and lodging. The first thing that you did when you arrived at new digs was to look at the comments in the visitors' book. If you saw that the person who had been there the previous week had written, "Quoth the Raven" you feared the worst because it was a quotation from Edgar Allen Poe's famous poem in which every verse ended with the words "Quoth the Raven, Never more."

There were some compensations for the hardships of Sunday travel. We did ourselves pretty well with picnic basket lunches of cold chicken, smoked salmon, pigeons, salads and quails eggs, washed down with a glass of wine. We read the Sunday papers and some of us tackled the Times crossword puzzle. I dreaded the moment when the fortunes were predicted under the signs of the zodiac. "What is your birthday Rona?" Answer, "September 16th". "Oh, that is Virgo!" This was the cue for some teasing. At first I was able to laugh at it, but as time went on it became rather a bore.

We travelled through some lovely scenery. England's green and pleasant land was comparatively unspoilt then, before the urban sprawl started encroaching on the countryside and on matinee days we had time to explore some of the historic towns we visited. On that tour our dates included, Torquay, Reading, Bath, Cheltenham, Manchester, Bradford, Hull, Birmingham, Cardiff and Leicester. I thought that Bath was the most beautiful city that I had ever seen. We were playing at the lovely little Theatre Royal and had time to explore the Abbey, the Baths and the Assembly Rooms.

I had only been on this tour for a short time when I found that our days had a regular pattern. There was the ritual of tea between the afternoon and evening shows on matinee days, usually taken in our dressing rooms but sometimes at the hotel, pub or digs where we were staying. Then there were nearly always drinks at a pub after the performance and sometimes there was a party at the end of the week.

I had to get used to the technical demands made by acting on areas of different sizes. One week we would be on a large stage, for example in Birmingham, and the next on Bath's pocket handkerchief sized one. We were always called to a rehearsal on the Monday to get used to the adjustments which had to be made because the distance between centre stage and the exits and entrances was different. I had to learn to count my steps so that I could time my exit lines properly. Lynn taught us that every scene must have a rhythm which went through the speaking of the lines, the pauses, the stage business, and the moves. "You mustn't miss a beat" he said. We had to be careful not to arrive at our exit too early, or, even worse, too late. He was a demanding but inspiring director.

As well as having to adjust to the different sized stages, we had to be aware of the different sizes of the auditoriums and had to be sure to project our voices to the back of the stalls and balconies and galleries. At the Monday run-through the Stage Manager was positioned in different parts of the auditorium to test if we could be heard easily. If we could not we were told in no uncertain terms to speak up. Would this discipline were practised today, then there wouldn't be so many complaints from audiences about inaudible actors. Lynn insisted that we spoke the line before the one on which he expected to get a laugh (the 'feed' line) very clearly. At the start of the tour I was not speaking these loudly enough. "Say it again" he would whisper urgently. This was a humiliating experience and I soon learnt to use more voice.

I found few references to the war while we were touring, but on 12th August I noted that the air raids had affected our business in Torquay. And when we were in Cheltenham there was a mock invasion by tanks and the show didn't go well there because people were preoccupied with fears of the possibility of this happening for real. When we were in Hull, four bombs were dropped during a heavy raid causing great devastation in the city centre. And in Bristol we saw the awful damage after another heavy raid.

The 'Thark' tour ended in Leicester and I went home to Derby. The family were horrified by my appearance. "You look like a whore's ghost" was my father's comment. And on the 17th December I wrote "Am still looking dreadfully pale and worrying Mimi to death." The tour had taken more out of me than I had realised, although a strong feeling of fellowship had been fostered in the cast and stage management even if not quite the camaraderie engendered by weekly rep.

I believe that our company was exceptionally lucky to have worked with Ralph Lynn; not only because of his brilliance as an actor in farce, but also because of the zest and energy he brought to both his on-stage and off-stage touring life. The playwright Ben Travers said that Ralph was the greatest comedy actor and the best timer of stage business that he had ever known and the dramatic critic James Agate once said to him, "You are no good to me. I can't criticise you. You know your job too well. You're far too perfect."

So ended my first experience of touring the provinces. Little did I know that when I set out on that tour it would be ten years before I appeared in the West End.

On the 21st December my agent send me a telegram telling me to come up to London the next day about a new play. I felt ill with excitement as I set off. Miriam Warner told me that I had been cast as the juvenile lead in a farce by Will Evans and Valentine, another of the Aldwych successes, 'Tons of Money' which was to go out on tour the following March with Lynn in his original part. I was deliriously happy and when I came out of Miriam's office London was bathed in sunshine.

So 1942 ended on a high note. I had survived my apprenticeship in the difficult art of farce and I had a new job waiting for me in 1943.

Photos of Ralph Lynn with Rona Laurie on tour

ENSA AND 'TONS OF MONEY'

Although the commercial tour of Thark was now over the company was committed to a short tour for ENSA,the Entertainments National Service Association nicknamed 'Every Night Something Awful'. Actually this was not really a fair criticism as some of the shows were very good. On 7th January I went up to Drury Lane Theatre for a brief refresher rehearsal. That afternoon I saw 'Yankee Doodle Dandy' at Warner Cinema. James Cagney was wonderful in it. Afterwards I went dancing with Dick at the Locarno.

8th January   We had another short rehearsal and a photo call. Then I had a drink at Carlton House with two of the Directors of the company, Barry O'Brien and Bernard Delfont, who was just beginning his career as a theatre manager.

The ENSA tour began on 11th January. We went down to a hostel in Frimley Green and then to Deepcut Camp for a performance to the Canadians. They were a noisy audience at first but calmed down later.From this base we played Cove and gave two more performances at Deepcut. On the 15th and 16th we were in Whitley and played to the Free French. They didn't understand most of it. I was able to get up to town to see the pantomime 'Mother Goose' at The Palladium. "Norman Evans gave a good performance. George Gee awful."

17th January   Over to Landguard House Hostel, and to the Garrison Theatre Aldershot for three shows. The opening one on the 18th was a great success and we took five curtain calls.

20th January	I went up to town and saw the film 'Casablanca'. Humphrey Bogart "superb".
21st January	To Bisley
22nd & 23rd January	Two shows at Longmore which went very well.
26th January	Up to town with Guy Fane who played Hook in 'Thark' and was later cast as the solicitor in 'Tons of Money'. We had drinks with Tod Slaughter (famous as Sweeny Todd, the demon barber of Fleet Street) and the theatre manager Jack Gatti. Afterwards we saw Disney's film 'Bambi', I loved it, especially the doe. On the 27th and 28th we gave two shows at Arbourfield and had drinks as usual in the Officers' Mess afterwards.
29th January	Over to Waverley Abbey for lunch with Mrs. Rupert Anderson, the Farnham fan "Delicious grouse".
31st January	Sunday. We travelled down to Folkestone and visited the Coastal Command.
1st February	Monday. Opening night. It went well.
3rd February	Saw the film, 'Queen Victoria'. "Anna Neagle needs producing"
5th February	Rehearsal with a new member of the cast. She was very nervous and pretty b… in the part poor dear.
6th February	Show not so good. New woman very bad.
7th February	Sunday. By train to Salisbury and our base on the Plain.
8th February	We gave a good show at Larkhill Garrison Theatre.
9th February	"I feel that my hands and arms are still dreadfully stiff"

11th February	Lunch at the Red Lion in Salisbury. To Officers' Mess after the show.
13th February	Last performance of tour. Met Binnie Hale afterwards.
14th February	Sunday. Back to London.

The response from the troops had ranged from real enthusiasm to obvious incomprehension from the Free French and boisterous reactions from the Canadians. But we had gained the experience of playing in contrasted venues. Now I was very excited about starting to rehearse 'Tons of Money'.

15th February	To see the film 'The Moon and Sixpence' and the play 'A Little Bit of Fluff' "My god, what squalor!" But, Henry Kendall "Fairly good".
16th February	First rehearsal of 'Tons of Money' at the Piccadilly Theatre. To see my agent in the afternoon and met the variety artist Wee Georgie Wood there.
17th February	Rehearsal at Piccadilly Theatre in the morning and in the Bedford pub in the afternoon. Was depressed because I couldn't get my part of 'Jean' at all.
18th February	A rehearsal at Bedford pub in the morning. I was in agony about Jean. Had lunch at Chinese restaurant. Afternoon off. To Simpson's in the Strand for tea. Then saw the review 'Fine and Dandy' at the Saville Theatre. Leslie Henson and Stanley Holloway were excellent in their sketch. Met Henson afterwards. To Marquis of Granby pub. Met Douglas Byng.
19th February	Rehearsal only in morning. Out to Barry O'Brien's wardrobe and tried on blue suit for Jean "Fairly alright."

20th February	Hair appointment with Frederic at Meg Scott's shop in South Moulton Street. I went to him every Monday when I was in work. To Teddington to see St. Mary's match against the Wasps. St Mary's beat them 9-3. I thought that Dick was on the way to falling in love with me. "Poor blighter!".

20th February — Hair appointment with Frederic at Meg Scott's shop in South Moulton Street. I went to him every Monday when I was in work. To Teddington to see St. Mary's match against the Wasps. St Mary's beat them 9-3. I thought that Dick was on the way to falling in love with me. "Poor blighter!".

23rd February — Lunch at Kettners. Tea at Rajah, Leicester Square. To news flick. Saw Mary Haley Bell's play 'Men in Shadow' starring John Mills (her husband) at the Lyric. "A rotten play." Saw John afterwards.

24th February — "Still not at all happy as Jean." Saw G. B. Shaw's 'The Doctor's Dilemma' at the Haymarket. "Vivien Leigh looked lovely, but her voice?"

27th February — Lunch at Scott's. Saw film 'You Were Never Lovelier'. Fred Astaire was particularly effective in one dance. Tea at Odenino's. Dinner with Dick at the 'Blue Horizon'.

1st March — First rehearsal at Prince's Theatre. Saw 'The Merchant of Venice' at the New Theatre Frederick Valk "Effective in scenes which called for a fast delivery".

2nd March — Saw Turgenev's 'A Month In The Country' at The St. James' Theatre. "Valerie Taylor awful and Michael Redgrave was a dim shadow of Gielgud." Dinner at the Brasserie Universelle. Rehearsal at Bedford pub. Lunch at Kettners. Saw film 'The Petrified Forest'. Air raid. We waited in the Globe foyer. There was a terrible disaster at Bethnal Green. A bomb fell on the tube station which was packed with people sheltering.

5th March	Rehearsed all day. "I shall be glad when the first night is over."
6th March	Sunday. Train to Cardiff. I had a comfortable room at the Royal Hotel.
7th March	Went round to the New Theatre. Saw I had good billing on the posters outside.
8th March	Show went well but I found it a bit of an anti-climax.
9th March	To see film 'The Silver Fleet' in the afternoon. "Very disappointing. Ralph Richardson rather smug?" After show went with Guy, Val Vaux, the Butler in 'Tons of Money' and Ralph to see Charlie Kunz's show at the Variety Theatre and met him back stage afterwards. When I was introduced the name Laurie didn't ring a bell with him and I did not remind him that when he was on tour in Derby and had a bout of lumbago he went to my father for radiant heat treatment. When he was lying on the bed the sun lamp above him broke and showered him with pieces of broken glass. My father told me afterwards that when he had been told that Charlie Kunz had booked in for an appointment he had expected to see two black men.
12th March	Pay day. Saw film 'A Yank at Eton' in the afternoon. "Child actor Freddie Bartholemew is finished I'm afraid."
13th March	Met Mayor of Cardiff, Captain Griffiths, an old sea-captain for sherry.
14th March	Sunday. Hell of a journey to Southsea. Left at half past eight and arrived at four twenty. I had booked in at the Queen's Hotel.

15th March	I thought that Southsea was a grand place. Lunch with Jasmine's mother 'Mugsie' at the Royal Naval Club".
16th March	Had my hair done at Handley's. "Seven shillings".
17th March	Guy, Ralph and I had drinks on H.M.S. Vernon and met the Commander.
18th March	Post-performance drinks in a private room at the hotel with some of the cast.
19th March	Met Clive Copestake the son of our family solicitor in Derby. He gave me sherry on his mine-sweeper.
20th March	Clive came round after the show. Drink at the King's pub.
21st March	Sunday. An easy journey to Brighton. Lunch at the Clarendon Hotel where I had booked. Heard Churchill's speech on the wireless. "There is no finer investment for any community than putting milk into babies." What would he have though of Margaret 'milk-snatcher' Thatcher? Sat on the seafront all afternoon. I loved my dressing room. Met H. F. Maltby who wrote the play 'The Rotters'. It was at Brighton that I discovered the delicious, but lethal, drink of Noilly Prat and Gin. This, accompanied by oysters in the bracing seaside air, made one feel good to be alive.
23rd March	Had a dozen Whitstable oysters at English's. Drink at the Pavilion with Guy and his wife Susan. During the evening performance Leslie Parker, who played Cousin George and I, fell through the settee and landed on the

	floor. We got, according to Ralph, the best laugh in the show. "Awful audience though."
24th March	Oysters at English's again. A dull matinee.
25th March	Had crab at English's. Saw a poor play "Peggy O'Neil"
26th March	To see the play 'The Pied Piper'. The children were excellent but Monty Woolley "looking like a Selfridges Father Christmas, overacted."
28th March	Sunday. Up to London. Lunch at the Grosvenor Victoria then off to Norwich. Arrived at Bell Hotel where I had booked.
29th March	Saw the films 'Desert Victory' about Libya and the eighth army and 'Sherlock Holmes in Washington'. There was an excellent reception for the opening night.
30th March	Drinks at Back's pub and met Captain Philip Back. The Verger took me around Norwich Cathedral. "It is Norman limestone and more beautiful than Salisbury inside. It has a lovely reliquary bridge".
31st March	To Strangers' club after the performance.
1st April	Business bad here. But we were knocking the play into shape. Drinks at Shakespeare pub opposite the theatre.
4th April	Sunday. "What a journey!" We left Norwich at eight a.m., missed our connection at Doncaster and had a nine hour's wait. The train didn't leave Doncaster until ten p.m. Then we had to change at York and Edinburgh and arrived in Glasgow at six o'clock the next morning.

5th April	Most of us were up at noon feeling alright. A good first night's performance.

5th April — Most of us were up at noon feeling alright. A good first night's performance.

6th April — Met Duncan McKinnon at the Piccadilly Hotel. His family owned the company and the rights to the famous Drambuie Liqueur. I wondered if he realised that I was the granddaughter of Eleanor Ross. When she was newly widowed she had handed over the recipe and the provenance of Drambuie to the McKinnon family. The label on the bottle today reads "An ancient Royal recipe, passed through generations and still made by the McKinnon family." Other advertisements describe how "The ancient and delicate liquor was first brought to Scotland in 1745, the year of the second Jacobite rebellion, and is claimed by the McKinnon family". This description, with no acknowledgement of the debt to the Ross family is greatly resented by us all to this day.

7th April — Duncan gave a champagne party for some of the cast.

8th April — Clare (who played the deaf aunt), Guy, Ralph and I went to a supper party with Duncan.

9th April — Show continued to go well.

10th April — I was sorry to be leaving Glasgow.

11th April — Felt rotten after mixing whisky and gin the night before. A trying train journey to Hull.

13th April — Saw touring production of 'Thunder Rock' "Frederick Valk very good."

16th April — Bought a handbag at Carmichael's shop.

18th April	Sunday. By train to Nottingham, went on to Derby for a brief visit to my family.
19th April	Lunch at Nottingham's County Hotel where I had booked. To see film 'Dark Journey'. Show went well.
20th April	Over to Derby for my sister Pauline's wedding to Jocelyn St John Baxter. She looked lovely. Rushed back to Nottingham for the matinee.
21st April	Oysters in the morning. Two shows.
22nd April	Mimi came over and was thrilled. She said that she really thought I'd do something on the stage. "A door is opening and your personality is coming through". This was welcome, and unexpected, praise. Saw film 'Random Harvest'.
24th April	Oysters in morning. To Black Boy Hotel for lunch. After evening performance some of us went to the historic pub 'The Trip To Jerusalem' which had been hewed out of the rock at the foot of the castle and we saw the dungeon 'Mortimer's Hole' at the back of the bar.
25th April	Sunday. Round to Black Boy to borrow a pound from Ralph. A good trip to Llandudno. Changed at Derby and Crewe (of course). I had booked in at a comfortable hotel.
26th April	Monday. A packed house for the first night but they coughed all the way through the third act.
27th April	To see film 'Tales of Manhattan' featuring Charles Laughton. "Awful coughing again in Act Three".

29th April	Met the cartoonist Bert Webster. He was very amusing.
30th April	Sat on the pier in the sun in the morning. Guy, Ralph and I had drinks with Webster. Lunch at Payne's Restaurant (underdone steak and asparagus.)
2nd May	Tedious journey to Bath. I had booked in at the Royal York Hotel.
6th May	Show went very well indeed this week.
9th May	An easy journey to Cheltenham. A good hotel. Successful first night.
12th May	Saw film 'Squadron Leader X'.
14th May	Ralph took Guy, Clare and me out to the Hop Pole Inn at Tewkesbury. It was a lovely sunny day and we sat in the grounds by the river. Days like this make touring a joy.
16th May	Sunday. Enjoyable picnic lunch (salmon). Back to London. Dick met me at Paddington.
17th May	Met Fay for lunch at La Coquille. Opening night at Streatham Theatre.
18th May	Saw agents John Glidden and Dorothy Mather. Lunch at the Lantern.
19th May	Lunch at the Ivy with William Armstrong, Clare and Ralph. There were a lot of celebrities there. To see J. B. Priestley's 'They Came to A City' at the Globe with Dick.
21st May	John Glidden came to the show and told me that he thought that I was very good. To the photographer John Vickers. Lillian Braithwaite was there. Lunch with Mugsie and Jasmine at Claridges (vin rosé). To see film 'La Fin Du Jour' "depressing". The Johnsons in to see the play. They enjoyed it.

22nd May — Tom Walls, Lynn's partner in the Aldwych farces was at the matinee. Dick came round at night and we danced at the Town Hall.

23rd May — Sunday. Off to Bradford. Picnic lunch (lobster). I had booked in at the Queen's Hotel.

24th May — Monday. Show was ok. "But Bradford - truly the comedian's grave".

26th May — Met Kingsley Lark of the Carl Rosa company. The houses were disappointing here.

30th May — Short journey to Burnley.

31st May — Appalling first night. One of the cast remarked, "They don't even seem to be enjoying it in their own way do they?"

1st June — Lousy matinee.

2nd June — Saw film 'The Man Who Came To Dinner'. Show still pretty awful.

4th June — Some of us went round an aircraft factory and had lunch there. Small audience at night.

5th June — Matinee pretty b…...

6th June — Up at ten a.m. Car to Todmorden Station where the Will Hay films were shot. Arrived at Newcastle. I had booked in at the Turk's Head opposite the Theatre Royal.

7th June — Monday. A good opening night, but I was mistiming.

8th June — Out to Jesmond Dene Gardens.

9th June — Saw film 'Commandos Fight At Dawn'. "Anna Lee shocking in it."

11th June — To Jesmond Dene again. Lovely flowers and sunshine.

12th June	Met George and Mrs Gee in hotel. A responsive evening audience, but I mistimed again.
13th June	Trying journey to Stockport. Had booked in at the White Lion.
14th June	Monday. Horrible stabbing pains. Managed to get through two shows. Was dreadfully sick at night.
15th June	Tummy still sore. Took castor oil. Had temperature of 102 degrees.
16th June	In bed all morning. Felt better for evening performance.
17th June	Was still a bit shaky. I realised that I must have had mussel poisoning from some I had eaten from a fish stall in a market at Newcastle.
18th June	Over to Liverpool for lunch with distinguished specialist Henry Cohen and Clare.
19th June	Listened in to The Derby. Walter Nightingale's horse 'Straight Deal' won. I got twenty five pounds which I put into my post office account. I now had sixty pounds there. There were very few at the matinee on that Derby Day and those who were there kept coughing. As we stood in the wings waiting for our cue, one of the cast said to me "Listen to Ralphie tripping the coughs". He always managed to time his comedy lines by putting in some stage business or making a gesture before them, waiting until he knew that he could be heard. The stage hands were listening to the race on their radios and giving us a running commentary. On the Sunday we

travelled to Preston. I had booked in at a pub, The George. I thought that Preston was a depressing place.

21st June

Monday. Saw film 'The Keeper of The Flame'. Opening night went well to our surprise.

22nd June

Saw a show 'Star-Spangled Rhythm.'.

23rd June

Over to Blackpool with Guy and Ralph. A lovely day. We went on the giant dipper.

28th June

Sunday. Was glad to leave those digs. Back to London. Dick met me.

28th June

Had hair done by Frederic. Tea at Arts Club with Clare. Then out to Croydon.

29th June

Saw John Glidden. He said he thought that I was too thin and advised me to go on a farm. "The devil!". Saw Dorothy Mather at H. M. Tennent's. Barry O'Brien came to show.

Looking back
on that 30th June

Saw Elsie Beyer at H. M. Tennents. Tea with the manager of the Croydon Theatre.

1st July

Went dancing with Dick at the Locarno at night.

2nd July

Helped at Youth Centre.

3rd July

Called at RADA and Spotlight.

4th July

Sunday. To Liverpool. Some of us were given special terms at the Adelphi Hotel. Met Espinosa. He was the Maitre De Ballet at the Royal Covent Garden Opera House and had actually worked for Henry Irving.

5th July	Monday. Espinosa in the audience. He told me that my performance was charming "I hope that he wasn't just being polite."
6th July	Saw film about the sinking of the Titanic, 'A Night To Remember'. Afterwards some of us went to Ma Eggerton's, a pub well known in the profession. Kingsley Lark was there and, we were told, two black marketeers. Met Dennis Noble, the actor and opera singer and John Mills in the hotel.
7th July	Supper with Henry Cohen. He said that I was "too thin for me".
8th July	To see 'Talk Of The Town' a musical comedy by Seymour Hicks. Afterwards met Sir Malcolm Sergeant in flirtatious mood.
11th July	Saturday. Round to Ma Eggerton's with Kingsley.
12th July	Sunday. Chicken picnic on train to London. Then on to Cambridge. Very late getting in. Had booked at the Blue Boar.
13th July	Monday. Performance went well. I had a lovely dressing room at the Arts Theatre. Lunch with Bill O'Brien. Drinks on the Arts' roof, afternoon on the river.
14th July	By boat on the Backs to St. John's college and moored under the willows.
15th July	Two performances. Felt dead tired but Cambridge was so peaceful and remote from the war.
16th July	Gorgeous hot day. Went on the river.
17th July	Sat in front of King's College between matinee and evening performance. End of

tour and a party. I stayed on afterwards for a few days and went with Frank Duncan and his wife (from Farnham Rep) to the service at King's College. The choir's singing was heavenly.

19th July	

19th July — Sat on the Backs in the afternoon. Then saw the play which followed us in at the Arts. It was an H.M. Tennent production 'Altitude 1400'. I was standing at the stage door when Richard Attenborough arrived. He called up the stairs to the dressing rooms. "Where is my wife?"He was newly married to Sheila Sim, one of the cast.

20th July — I met my old flame Clifford Evans with his wife Hermione Hannen for a few seconds. Strangely enough I made no comment about this in the diary. To the Arts for a coffee with Dulcie Gray and John Byron. Had lunch there and went on river with Dulcie and Kitty Black.

21st July — To Newmarket races. Backed successfully but poor prices. I only got one and three pence back on my ten shilling outlay. Up to town to Gloucester Road digs. Dinner at Fay's.

22nd July — To Spotlight. They were very encouraging and said that I was doing good work.

23rd July — Went to audition for a play by Mabel and Dennis Constanduros, 'Acacia Grove'. Didn't get the part but it was not my cup of tea anyway. Met Jack at the Aero Club. Dinner at Hatchet's where we danced and then on to the Brevet Club. He took me home and told me that I took my work too seriously.

24th July — Saturday. Saw Elsie Beyer at Tennent's. Lunch at Lantern then up to Derby.

25th July   The family thought that I was still looking pale.

From the end of the 'Tons of Money Tour' on 17th July up to the 17th August I was job hunting and met Terence Rattigan and Anthony Asquith (both queer). Later I went for a part in Rattigan's 'While the Sun Shines' but didn't get it. I spent a few days fishing at Dove Cottage that month. Had a rise from a brown trout on the 10th August but no catch.

There was a welcome weekend break on the 13th August when I went with Dick to the Packhorse Hotel. We played tennis and bathed. I succeeded in falling into the river, fully dressed, much to the amusement of everyone on the terrace. On the 15th August we bathed and went out in the canoe. Dick said "Don't get married or engaged or anything will you?"

Portrait of Rona Laurie

1943-4 A CRUSHING BLOW

Is your honeymoon really necessary?

On the 17th I was told about the possibility of a part in a new play 'Is Your Honeymoon Really Necessary?' This over-long title was an adaptation of the wartime slogan designed to put people off travelling: "Is Your Journey Really Necessary?" I went up to town. Lunched at Kettners. Flanagan and Allen were there. Called for a script of the play at Geoffrey Sutton's office. One of the two leading girls' parts, Rosemary, was wonderful.

18th August	Read Rosemary at the Ambassador's Theatre. Sutton said that he liked it and that I could play the part if he could get a star man. "My god, I hope so." Little did I know then how he was going to treat me. Lunched with him and Ralph at La Coquille. Saw the review 'Sweet and Low' at the Ambassador's. "Hermione Gingold very good". Back to Derby and out to the cottage with my father for the night.
21st August	He fished in the morning and caught a two-pounder which I cooked in oatmeal for supper.
22nd August	Saw the touring company in Emlyn Williams' 'Night Must Fall' with him in his original part. Met Kynaston Reeve who played the judge.
24th August	Reeve came to our house in the evening and I had a long talk with him.

28th August	Saw the film 'I Married A Witch'.
31st August	Had a message to say that I had to go up to London on September 2nd to see my agent, and that Enid Stamp Taylor had been engaged for the other girl's part. Saw 'Old Chelsea' starring Richard Tauber. My cryptic diary comment was "back of the throat" referring to his singing voice I suppose. I met him backstage. A second reading of 'Honeymoon' at the Ambassador's. Lunch at La Coquille afterwards with Enid, Ralph, Sutton and Henry Hewitt. He was cast as the solicitor. Went to dress designer in Cavendish Square.
3rd September	Called for my contract at Sutton's office to find him in a state. He told me that I must rehearse before they could decide whether I could play the part that I was reading (Rosemary). This was <u>hell.</u> With hindsight I should have suspected that I wouldn't get the part but I didn't foresee, at that stage, that Sutton would give it to his girlfriend Betty Rogers (who later changed her first name to Faith). Lunch at Chinese restaurant and then saw film 'Coney Island' starring Betty Grable.
4th September	Met Dick at St. Mary's. We went to Lord's. A disappointing match. Fishlock batted well, Peebles fielded badly. Met Bill O'Brien there.
6th September	Evening with Jack. We went to the Gay Nineties Club, The Mayfair, Pruniers and The Brevet. (The energy I must have had).
8th September	Met Barry O'Brien at his office. Saw a lovely film, 'Heaven Can Wait' then went on to see Enid Bagnold's 'Lottie Dundas at the Vaudeville. "Terrible and Sybil Thorndyke

	not good. Ann Todd moved well and looked lovely but oh her acting!"
9th September	Lunch at Lantern. Met d'Oyly-John the painter who made a dead set at me. Saw Congreve's 'Love for Love' at the Phoenix. A terrific show with Gielgud, Yvonne Arnaud and Leslie Banks.
10th Septmber	Met d'Oyly-John for walk in the park. An odd man. Lunch at Sheekey's, then saw 'Watch On The Rhine' (for the second time). A star-studded cast, Walbrook, Wynyard, Seyler, Judy Campbell. Off to Pamela's. She met me at Newbury.
11th September	Walk on Plain in the morning. Blackberried after tea. Moonlight and very happy.
12th September	Sunday. To church. I was very sleepy. Walking in the afternoon and we managed to finish the Times crossword puzzle.
13th September	Walk on Plain. Into Newbury to see film. 'Tutankhamun' at Studio One, featuring Annie Vernay and Suzy Prim. Got back to London in late evening.
14th September	Had lunch with Keith Scott's girlfriend at the English Speaking Union. She told me that Dick adored me. Out with Jack to Berkeley Buttery and Mayfair Club.
15th September	Lunch at Kettners. Saw Deanna Durbin film.
16th September	My birthday. (27)

Rehearsal at Ambassadors. I read and they seemed pleased. I thought I'd keep the part but was worried about Faith Rogers. I suspected that Sutton was pushing her. Lunch at Chinese Restaurant.

17th September	Rehearsals going well. Met Sutton and Ralph for lunch at La Coquille.

17th September — Rehearsals going well. Met Sutton and Ralph for lunch at La Coquille.

18th September — Out to the Johnsons. Saw film 'Background to Danger' with Dick. I noted that I *couldn't* feel excited about him. What a nuisance.

20th September — Good rehearsal at Ambassador's. I believed that it was all right about the part.

21st September — Rehearsals going well.

22nd September — Rehearsal at Duke of Argyle. Difficult scene with Enid and Henry so I went home and slogged at it.

23rd September — The blow fell. Sutton told me that I was "too young, sweet and gentle, for the part". Instead he offered me a contract to play the minute part of the Lady's Maid (one of the two maids), to understudy the two leading parts and to stage-manage. Faith Rogers, as I had feared, was to play Rosemary. I was heartbroken, felt ill, had an awful night and didn't sleep until three a.m. I think now that I should have refused to sign that contract. But I had no other job to go to, not even the prospect of one. And, on the other hand, I enjoyed touring and there were good friends of mine in the 'Honeymoon' company with whom I'd worked before.

24th September — Felt in fighting mood. Sent notes to Elsie Beyer and Dan O'Neill. Wrote to Robert Donat. At least I showed some spirit. Hazel's boyfriend Vernon Kelso was sweet to me when I told him what had happened on the next day, as was Frederic my hairdresser.

Sunday	Felt quite cheerful but my blood was up about Honeymoon.
27th September	The rehearsals were pretty awful. I hated all the inevitable hanging about.
29th September	Rehearsal at the Duke of York's Theatre. Lunch at Sheekey's. I got very bored rehearsing,
30th September	Lunch at Kettners. Saw Eric Maschwitz and Ronald Jeans review 'Flying Colours' at the Lyric. Douglas Byng and Binnie Hale "Both excellent."
1st October	Rehearsed all morning at the Duke of Argyle's. Over to the Westminster Theatre to see the producer and actor Jack Minster who was charming and told me to keep on plugging at Robert Donat.
2nd October	Met Dick at the Castle's pub. Dinner with him and Tommy Kemp.
6th October	To Cambridge Theatre and saw Robert Donat in his dressing room. He was playing Captain Shotover in Bernard Shaw's 'Heartbreak House'. As expected he was charming but I was not very hopeful about the possibility of him giving me a job. Met Basil Radford and Ralph at Sheekey's. We had oysters. Saw Rose Franken's 'Claudia' at the St. Martin's Theatre. Joyce Redman was very good in name part. Out with Jack in evening to Wings and Brevet clubs. There was an air raid on.
7th October	Another b.... rehearsal. How I resented that position. Lunch at Gows with Vernon, Hazel and Ralph.

8th October

Saturday. Over to Teddington, St. Mary's beat OCTU. Tommy Kemp was playing. Then to Cables pub. There was some ill feeling because St. Mary's rugger team was mostly composed of medical students who were exempted from the call-up. They were nicknamed 'The Professionals'. To Cambridge for the start of the tour. Booked in at the Blue Boar. Dress rehearsal. Not good from the stage management point of view. But my costume was a great success. Vernon said that the maids were more attractive than the Principals. Hazel was playing the other maid. Thank God. "I may make something of my part if I am given a few more lines." Supper at the Arts Theatre.

11th October

Opening night. As I expected, it was a trying day. Line rehearsal in the morning. Show went very well indeed. A success. Party for the Company afterwards. I had been on the book as prompter all evening and of course was very upset about not playing Rosemary.

12th October

Another line rehearsal in the morning. Bought Henry, Hubert and Ralph drinks. I found Faith most trying in her mannerisms. Enid Stamp Taylor and her 'old man' boyfriend gave the cast a party.

13th October

Photocall. Then dinner with smarmy Geoffrey. I felt all on edge. Supper with Hazel and Vernon at the Arts Theatre. They were very comforting.

14th October

Two shows again. I enjoyed dinner at the Festival Restaurant. The best food in Cambridge.

15th October	We were taken round the ADC 'Amateur Dramatic Club'. They have a lovely lighting system. On river in the afternoon. The Backs looked beautiful with the leaves turning. Chatted with Henry in the Blue Boar after show.
17th October	Returned to London.
18th October	Out to Croydon. Dick saw the performance and depressed me about the size of my part.
19th October	Felt profoundly depressed and asked myself if I could continue to endure 'Honeymoon'. Air raid warning at night.
20th October	Another despairing entry in the diary. "I really can't go on like this."
21st October	Had a pretty sickening lunch with Sutton and his accountant at Scott's. It was a waste of oysters and champagne. With Dick to see Noel Coward's 'Blithe Spirit' at the Piccadilly Theatre. Kay Hammond brilliant as the first wife Elvira.
22nd October	Saw the actor and producer Dennis Arundell. I read the part of Nancy, the maid in Patrick Hamilton's 'Gaslight'. He told me that I was "very near what he wanted" (some comfort). Saw Kitty Black. Lunch with Faith at The Interval Club, "it was pretty b….., but kind of her".
23rd October	Saturday. I found Faith's performance on and off the stage maddening.
24th October	Good journey up to Bradford. I had booked in at the Alexandra Hotel and had a nice room. Drinks at famous pub 'Auntie's'.

25th October	Monday opening night. A warm reception.
27th October	Out by taxi to Ye Old Ragnold's Inn, Queensbury for lunch. Show went very well indeed. "I can't like Faith's performance and I am sure that it is not sour grapes".
28th October	Pretty awful understudy rehearsal. Then two shows.
30th October	Drinks with Hubert at the New Inn. Heard from home that I had an audition with H. M. Tennent's.
31st October	Sunday. Travelled to Nottingham. I had booked in at the George Hotel.
1st November	Oysters at the bar opposite the theatre. Show went well.
2nd November	Over to Derby and back for evening performance. Rather dull party at the County Hotel.
3rd November	Understudy rehearsal. Got fur coat. Really lovely. Opossum. £43.17 from Griffin and Spalding's.
4th November	My parents came over for dinner with Ralph and me at the George. They were depressing about my part in 'Honeymoon', and told me to leave the show for something better. Of course this upset me. All three of us back to Derby by car.
5th November	Lunch at home. My parents were sympathetic.
6th November	We did £1250 of business here.
7th November	Back to London, then on to Chatham where I had booked in at the Sun Hotel. Delicious point steak for supper.

8th November	Hotel was <u>most</u> comfortable. Poor house for opening night. Geoffrey Sutton came down for lunch with Mr Smith and his secretary.
10th November	Over to Rochester and saw round the castle. Spoke to Geoffrey about my billing.
12th November	Up to town and to the Globe theatre for Tennent audition. I spoke the sonnet 'When forty winters shall besiege thy brow' and followed it with a speech from George Bernard Shaw's 'Fannie's First Play'. The reaction was soulless and cold-blooded. They might have been dummies sitting in the stalls. Saw news-flick. Show rather slow. Afterwards had drinks with some of the Navy personnel who were stationed at Chatham. "An old man pawed me."
14th November	Journey from Chatham to Southsea. Picnic of goose on train. Had an attractive room at the Queen's Hotel on the front.
15th November	Also had a good dressing room and I was given a new little comedy scene in the play.
17th November	Show went wonderfully well here.
18th November	Understudy rehearsal, then we all went to a dance in the Town Hall.
19th November	I phoned Mugsie (Jasmine's mother) and she told me to look on their house at Fareham as a home.
20th November	Lovely party on board the Queen Elizabeth. I went up on the Compass Bridge. I enjoyed being surrounded by the Navy and had an 'on' day.

21st November	Sunday. Pretty fiendish journey to Cheltenham. Out to Rosslyn Manor Country Club where some of us had been given a reduced tariff.
26th November	Mr. Simpson, the manager of the theatre, said that I ought to have been playing Rosemary.
27th November	Hazel and her Pekinese 'Ming' came over for the day.
29th November	By bus to Stratford-On-Avon to Swan's Nest Hotel. Show only fair. Hazel and I shared a dresser and a dressing-room. Drinks with Barbara Curtis (wardrobe mistress at the theatre).
1st December	Had understudy rehearsal. Vernon arrived after the matinee. It was good to see him. We sat up talking at Swan's Nest till lateish.
2nd December	Understudy rehearsal in theatre bar. Met Vernon, Hazel and Hubert at the Plough Pub. We all got a bit merry. After performance to the Dirty Duck Pub, the actors' name for the Black Swan. Robert Atkins was there.
3rd December	Good houses for the show.
4th December	Saturday. Note from Enid to say that she really felt rather ill and was warning me in case I had to go on. I rushed to the theatre, went through her lines and tried on her costumes. As I was very slim and she was quite buxom her cami-knickers were far too big for me and had to be safety-pinned round me for the matinee. After lunch had a quick run-through with Henry Hewitt. I got through the matinee ok except for the first act when I was speaking too quietly. Studied the part

between shows and was much better in the evening. Ralph was pleased and mentioned me in his curtain speech. The audience were very kind. It transpired that Enid who had been up to London and was travelling back, crossing the Avon to the Swan's Nest Hotel fell into the river. She was weighed down by her two heavy suitcases and she had developed a chill.

5th December   Up late. Felt whacked but went out for drinks with Hubert, Ralph and Barbara. People had been very nice about my performance on the Saturday night. Of course it had been a great thrill acting on the stage of the famous Memorial Theatre. Lunch at the Dirty Duck then off on the afternoon train en-route for Southport. We had to change trains at Birmingham, then we had a long journey to Liverpool Exchange Station, arriving in the black-out. Then we caught the train to Southport and didn't get in until eleven-thirty.

6th December   Felt very tired. No word from Enid so I phoned her at lunchtime and she told me that she was not playing that week. I wrote in my diary, "I am a lucky person to have this chance; even if it is not Rosemary it is the other lead". Studied lines in the afternoon. Early to theatre. I had the Number One dressing room and a dresser. Show pretty b..... that night. My voice was too high and the lighting was awful.

7th December   Felt exhausted but walked down Lord Street and looked at the shops. I gave a much better performance and had a good notice. "Miss. Laurie is to be congratulated on her valiant work in a part that demands the most exact casting" and "Miss. Laurie plays up, like a good trouper, Yvonne, the wife that was."

8th December   I felt that Yvonne was gradually improving.

9th December   All went smoothly. I felt now that I was on the right tack and was more relaxed.

10th December   Felt very tired and fluey, but the digs were excellent with lovely coal fires and good food. I was gradually building up the part of Yvonne and enjoying it.

11th December   We took £299 that night - the biggest house yet. I was deadbeat afterwards. This was my last performance as Yvonne.

12th December   Up and out of the digs in the moonlight for early train back to London. Changed at Wigan. McKenzie Ward was on the train. I had seen him in The Wind and The Rain' years before, playing opposite Celia Johnson and had never forgotten his performance - and hers.

13th December   Hair appointment with Frederic. To H.M. Tennent's and saw Kitty Black. Then to Firth Shepherd's office. They were not seeing anyone until after Christmas. Out to Wimbledon Theatre. Enid had resumed her part. Heard that Geoffrey had refused the offer of the Comedy Theatre for the 'Honeymoon' show to open on Boxing Day. I thought that he was mad. Had drinks with David.

14th December   Queued for tickets for the film 'For Whom the Bell Tolls'. Met David at Dutch Oven for lunch. He practically proposed again and gave me five clothing coupons. In the afternoon I went to the Westminster Theatre and saw Oscar Wilde's 'An Ideal Husband'. Roland Culver was brilliant and Irene Vanbrugh very good. Clare came out to Wimbledon and told me that I would always fall on my feet. Robertson 'Bunny' Hare, Basil Redford and Ralph's brother Sydney all in to the show.

15th December   Met Ralph and Hubert at Kettner's. Oysters at lunch. Saw 'For Whom the Bell Tolls'.

16th December   The two performances seemed endless. It was a great comfort to have Dick waiting for me at the station when I got back at night.

17th December   Met Hubert at the Green Room Club for a drink. (Now a conceited entry). The President of the West End Managers' Association told Woody how attractive he thought I was.

18th December   Fay and her two children Toby and Toppet (Teresa) arrived at the Matinee and Fay said that my performance was finished. (I hoped that she meant this as a compliment).

19th December   To Staines for lunch at the Packhorse Inn. We chalked the numbers on the chairs, ready for the evening concert, which was a star-studded affair, given for charity and featured Hermione Baddeley, Leslie Henson, Joyce Grenfell, Adelaide Hall, Kenneth Horne, Richard (Stinker) Murdoch and Hutch. Party afterwards. Bed at 3 a.m.

20th December   Up to town. Felt very sleepy. Met Hazel for drinks at the Salted Almond. Dinner at the Arts Theatre. Saw the Lunts in 'There Shall Be No Night' by Robert Sherwood at the

Aldwych. Lynn Fontanne looked exquisite. Alfred Lunt was superb with a new technique - a good deal of back to the audience. The headline in a review of the revival was "Alfred Lunt's back".

21st December   Lunch with Jack at Simpson's. Train back to Derby.

24th December   Listened in to Gracie Fields singing 'Sally' and 'Ave Maria'.Terrific.

25th December   Christmas Day. After supper we listened in to Robert Donat's beautiful reading from Tennyson's 'In Memoriam'.

'Ring out, wild bells, to the wild sky,
The flying cloud, the frosty light;
The year is dying in the night;
Ring out, wild bells, and let him die.
Ring out the old, ring in the new,
Ring happy bells across the snow;
The year is going, let him go;
Ring out the false, ring in the true.'

27th December   Boxing Day. Dora Patey and I went over to Leicester to see the Barbarians play Leicester Tigers. Hollis had a good game. He reminded me of Alex Obolensky.

31st December   Down to Claygate with David. We went to the dance at Oakland's Park Hotel near Weybridge. I wore my white satin dress. It was all very pre-war and great fun. But people had to carry their ration books into dinner. I had to fob David off. His parents Brigadier and Mrs Hull were there. Both very nice. Bed at 2:00a.m.

So ended 1943 - a year of mixed fortunes for me. First there had been the short ENSA tour, followed by the longer engagement in 'Tons Of Money'. Then I had been out of work for two months before the crushing blow of losing the part which I had been rehearsing in 'Is Your Honeymoon Really Necessary?' to Sutton's girlfriend Faith. However there had been some compensation in having to go on for Enid in the other leading part Yvonne, for ten performances. I had got over my disappointment but never came to terms with combining the part of the Lady's Maid with understudying the two principal female parts and stage managing. Then the Sunday journeys had ranged from short to exhausting ones with constant delays and changes and late arrivals. On the plus side there had been the experience of travelling through beautiful scenery and enjoying delicious picnic lunches. I had become used to acting on different sized stages and to different audiences and I had, as well, made some good friends in the Company and had met some interesting people. The year 1943 had been a roller-coaster journey, but I had survived.

✂XV✂
1944

THE LAST TOUR

My engagement in 'Honeymoon' was not yet over. There was a second tour going out at the end of January.

1st January	Saw Ben Travers' play 'She Follows Me About' at the Garrick Theatre.
16th January	Met Wilfrid Hyde-White
17th January	Started 'Honeymoon' rehearsals with Lilli Palmer's sister, the replacement for Enid Stamp Taylor who had died in an accident at the end of 1943. I had now resumed my part of Marie, the Lady's Maid.
18th January	Lunch at Bentley's. To see Cinderella at His Majesty's in a box with Vernon, Hazel and Hubert. Met Evelyn (Boo) Laye and Arthur Askey afterwards.
22nd January	Had lunch with David - not a success. Saw film of 'Carnet de Bal'. Out with Evelyn and Ross to their local pub the Lamb and Flag.
24th January	Rehearsal. To Hatchets with Jack.
26th January	Lunch with George Smith. He had now taken over the management of 'Honeymoon'. Saw the film 'Halfway to Heaven' with Bryan.

27th January	Saw Stanley Lupino in the 'Love Racket' at the Victoria Palace. Arthur Askey was brilliant. Met him afterwards.
29th January	To Park Lane office. Good dinner at Scott's with Smith. He seemed interested in me. I let him kiss me - fool! To Teddington. Met Dick and Ian. St. Mary's rugger team lost to Cambridge University. To Castles pub. Air raid.
30th January	Sunday. Off to Brighton for the start of second 'Honeymoon' tour. This took us there again and I enjoyed oysters and champagne at English's.
31st January	Met J. Baxter Somerville, theatrical manager. Ralph introduced me, not very tactfully, to Winifred Shotter, the original Kitty, the part which I'd played in 'Thark'.
1st and 2nd February	Oysters at English's. Smith and Sutton in to see the show. Went around a whisky distillery with some of the cast.
3rd February	Hubert down for matinee. George Patey at evening show.
4th February	Again, oysters at English's. Saw film 'The Sky's the Limit'.
5th February	Explored The Lanes and bought a Pinchbeck seal for thirty shillings.
6th February	Sunday. Long journey to Hull. Picnic of wood pigeon.
7th February	Went round Carmichael's shop. A smooth performance.
8th February	Drink with Sparkie, our stage manager and Ralph. Saw film 'The Four Feathers'.

11th February	Some of the cast were invited to drink champagne with Santiago, the theatre manager.
12th February	Champagne party in the morning.
13th February	Sunday. Easy journey to Huddersfield. I'd booked in at the George Hotel.
14th - 19th February	It was a pleasant week. All going well but I was still upset about Rosemary.
20th February	Sunday. We had a nightmare journey to Leicester from 10:00am until 9:20pm, I'd booked in at the Bell Hotel.
21st February	Faith late in to the theatre so I went on for Rosemary. Ralph and Sparkie were pleasant about it but I was shaky in the last act. I had now played three out of the four female parts in the play. An uneventful week apart from that.
27th February	Another ghastly journey - twelve hours, but I had booked in at a good pub in Hanley.
28th February	Opening night. A success.
1st March	I heard that Philip had been killed at the Anzio Beach-Head. "What a waste."
2nd March	Understudy rehearsal. Geoffrey came down to see the show. While we were in the Potteries in Hanley some of us were taken round two china works, on the third to the Moorcroft (where we met Mr. Moorcroft himself) and the next day to the Doulton where I was given two china figures.
5th March	Sunday. A lovely journey to Glasgow. Picnic lunch of pigeons' eggs. I had booked in at the Beresford hotel.

9th March	Saw two famous Scottish character actors, Will Fyffe and Harry Gordon in their 'Old People' sketch in the pantomime. They were superb and the Dagenham Girl Pipers impressed.
12th March	Sunday. Through wonderful scenery to Chester. Met Leslie French, well-known for his performances as Puck, Ariel, and Feste. There is a sculpture of him by Eric Gill on the front of Broadcasting House.
17th March	Walked all around the walls at sunset. Felt depressed.
19th March	Sunday. Up early and off to Morecambe where I booked in at the Royal Hotel.
22nd March	I really found it impossible to like Faith.
23rd March	Sparkie and I saw the touring production of Rose Franken's 'Claudia'. Pamela Brown very good in name part.
25th March	We were shown around the Souplex Factory and I was given a nice set of razor blades. Had shrimp tea with Sparkie.
26th March	Up early. Back to London en route for yet another visit to Brighton. I had booked in at the Dudley Hotel, Hove.
27th March	Met Donald Wolfit and Rosalind Iden who had seen the show.
28th March	Walked to Ovingdean. Sat on the front. Met Sid Walker.
30th March	To the Ship Hotel for lunch with Ralph and Faith.

31st March	I was on the up and up. Lobster lunch. Saw film 'Rage in Heaven'. Ingrid Bergman 'grand'. Drinks with Jack Keats, manager of the Theatre Royal.
1st April	Tea with Hubert, Ralph and Enid. She was complimentary about my stage make-up.
2nd April	Sunday. Long journey to Cardiff. To Royal Hotel.
3rd April	Was told that the management had queried Faith for the London production.
5th April	Variety Theatre programme at the New Theatre. "Sid Walker awful and Leslie Hatton, worse".
9th April	Sunday. Easy journey to Torquay. Cold tripe for picnic lunch. Delicious. The manager of the Imperial Hotel had given some of us a cut-price for the week; seven guineas.
10th April	Ronald Simpson, who was in the audience, liked me. I danced for an hour and a half with Jacques, a Free French sub-lieutenant. They were stationed in Torquay.
11th April	Danced with Jacques again.
13th April	We were taken over their ships by the Free French. Back to London. End of tour. I had mixed feelings about it. My first tour in farce, 'Thark' had begun in Torquay, and my last one in 'Honeymoon' ended there. We had had particularly long journeys this time but I had been lucky in my choice of hotels and digs and had enjoyed some lovely, sunny days. Most importantly I'd had a chance of going on for Rosemary, even if it had been

only for one performance, and now I was back in London job hunting.

16th April   Back in London, Dick met me. Saw 'Black Vanities' at the Victoria Palace.

19th April   Over to Westminster Theatre. Jack Minster very pleasant. Saw Anna Neagle rehearsing.

20th April   Bus strike. Had lunch with Smith at Scott's.

21st April   To Westminster Theatre again. Jack Minster said "You don't want to understudy". Afraid I was tactless about Anna Neagle. In the afternoon saw Donald Wolfit's 'Lear' at the Scala Theatre. Sat on a hard wooden chair, entranced throughout. It was only a medium company but Wolfit was mesmerising, a tremendous voice in the storm and capturing the pathos in his final scene with Cordelia. I have never forgotten the way in which he spoke the lines

"Why should a dog, a horse, a rat have life
And thou no breath at all?"

as he knelt beside her dead body. I didn't cry during the performance but sat there with an aching throat and stumbled out at the end, completely drained emotionally. I realised then what the term "catharsis" meant - a purging of the emotions. I had to retire to bed for the rest of the day. But it had been a glorious experience. I recently read James Agate's review of Wolfit's 'Lear'. "I say deliberately that his performance on Wednesday was the greatest piece of Shakespeare acting I have ever seen since I have been privileged to write for the 'Sunday Times." I had been in good company in my assessment.

22nd April

Out to Richmond for the seven-aside Rugby competition which St. Mary's won amid great excitement. Party afterwards.

24th April

After lunch with Hubert and Ralph we saw the film 'A Guy Named Joe' starring Spencer Tracey. "Very sad".

25th April

Round the agents in the morning. Supper at the Dutch Oven.

26th April

Job hunting again. Lunch at Café Royal. Saw Arthur McCrae's 'Something In the Air' at the Palace Theatre, starring Jack Hulbert and Cicely Courtneidge.

27th April

Had tea with them the next day. Met Yvonne Arnaud in her dressing room at the Phoenix where she was appearing as Mrs Frail in Congreve's 'Love for Love'. She was doing her feet!

28th April

Another day job hunting. Auditioned unsuccessfully for 'Lilac Time' a new play with Schubert's music.

2nd May

Lunch at Sheekey's. Saw 'This Was A Woman' starring Sonia Dresdel at the Comedy Theatre. With Jack to Berkley in the evening.

3rd May

Saw Roland Pertwee's 'Pink String and Ceiling Wax' at the Duke of York's.

4th May

Went to the Apollo Theatre for opening night of Priestley's 'How Are They At Home?'

6th May

Firth Shepherd telephoned my agent offering me an understudy job in the new production that he was putting on at the Savoy Theatre, after a week's try-out in Blackpool. It was

Frederick Lonsdale's 'The Last of Mrs. Cheyney.' My Principals were to be Madge Compton (Mrs Wynton), Frances Rowe (Joan) and Ann Firth (Mary). I accepted the job thankfully and gratefully.

8th May   Watched 'Cheyney' rehearsal.

LONDON UNDER FIRE. 'The Last of Mrs. Cheyney'

So at last I had arrived in the West End, albeit only as an understudy, but with a prestigious management. And I had entered into a lifestyle which I had only partially experienced up until then.

The West End Theatre in those days (before Television and exposure in the Media) was a closed community of producers, directors, agents, playwrights, actors and actresses. Binkie Beaumont of HM Tennent's management reigned supreme and Firth Shepherd was powerful also. If you were lucky enough to be enjoying the run of a play, you went to parties given by the casts of other productions, or entertained them in your own theatre. My social life 'took off' and my diary records numerous lunches and late suppers after the show. And then there were the clubs, the Stage Golfing Society, the Green Room and the Mayfair for example. There were favourite restaurants where you were always meeting fellow artists, stars, writers and designers. The Ivy was the most distinguished, but the Café Royal, the Ritz, Scotts, Simpsons, Sheekeys, Gows, Kettners and La Coquille were also popular with us. As the Savoy Theatre was adjacent to the hotel I was sometimes taken to the Savoy Grill. When we were out of work we would go to Lyon's Cornerhouse or the Brasserie Universelle. The theatre remained open throughout the war as did the Windmill. We had our share of raids and a bomb on the Embankment shattered the hotel windows. During air raids we used to take refuge in our dressing room wardrobe cupboards, but I can't think that they would have offered much shelter from a direct hit. One evening during the performance there was a particularly loud explosion just as Jack Buchanan as Lord Dilling was opening a bottle of champagne. His next line was "Now what could be quieter than that?" our audiences sat stoically through air raid warnings and I don't remember many people ever leaving the auditorium.

10th May During the rehearsal period I was fascinated by watching Tony Guthrie's direction of the cast as he stood in the stalls of the Savoy - a tall, lean figure making loud comments. I remember him saying to the seasoned actress Athene "No tricks now Athene". She opened her eyes wide in mock-surprise "I don't know what you mean, Tony". But she did.

I sometimes had to fill in for any absentee and in early rehearsals read the part of Mrs Wynton as my Principal Madge Compton had come late to rehearsals. One particular morning after we had been working hard at a scene and had thankfully come to the end of it, Tony called out cheerfully, "Now let's all try it again in a different way". We could have killed him.

This was our leading man Jack Buchanan's first appearance in a straight play after thirty years in musical comedy. It was evident during rehearsals that he and his leading lady Coral Brown had fallen passionately in love. The onstage chemistry between them was obviously felt offstage as well. One day, during the run I remember Athene Seyler who had been an amused spectator of the affair saying to me "Our leading lady and leading man have been riding in a taxi round Hyde Park between the matinee and tonight's performance. She came back with her hair tumbled halfway down her back." But I was caught up in the romance. They were tall, darkly handsome and obviously deeply in love.

Years later in 1983, Coral played herself in Alan Bennett's play 'An Englishman Abroad'. In the scene with Alan Bates, who was playing the spy Guy Burgess, when they were in his flat listening to the record of Buchanan singing 'Who Stole my Heart Away' Bates watched Coral's reaction and asked if she had known him. "I almost married him" she said. Coral was notorious in the profession for her use of bad language and her wit. 'Coral Brown' stories, some of them apocryphal, went the rounds. The cast had got used to this during rehearsals but the stage hands during the run were physically shaken by her offstage comments. At one matinee I remember standing in the wings as Coral, looking exquisite in her Motley-designed costume, gazed out of the window muttering to us "They are a lot of bastards out front". She and I got on very well. While the play was on the pre-London tryout at Blackpool she asked me to take her miniature black poodle Blossom for a walk every day. This caused me some embarrassment when passers-by called out jeering remarks such as "Call that a dog? Or half a dog!". As a minor member of the company I had the task of going round the dressing rooms collecting money for the Red Cross. This was not without its hazards. I remember one particular occasion which made me blush. When I knocked on Coral's dressing room door she opened it stark naked. "Come in Rona". This was shocking enough, but when the door was closed I saw three airmen sitting on a bench against the wall. They were more embarrassed than I was. I ought to have been warned because the week before I had come across Athene leaning against the wall in the wings. "What's the matter Athene?" "I have just had an awful experience. I knocked at Coral's dressing-room door, she opened it, stark naked and said "Come in Athene" then Firth appeared from the inner-room saying, "Yes, come in and have a drink Athene.""

11th May	No rehearsal. Into agent Gordon Harbord's office. Saw Reginald Beckwith's 'A Soldier For Christmas' at Wyndhams starring Trevor Howard.
12th May	Got frock from Polly Spruce.
13th May	Morning rehearsal. To Lord's with Dick. Keith Miller made ninety one for the Civil Defence. Read in for Madge Compton at rehearsal.
16th May	There was some question of my playing the part, but I was considered to be too young. Tony Guthrie was sweet and explained the

situation to me in a letter which I had from him at the end of the London rehearsals. "Thank you for your very nice note... I too hope we may work together shortly. Your helpful bits of filling in at rehearsal made me feel sure you can act. I am sorry that neither of the two parts available in Cheyney were quite up your street."

19th May	Rehearsed all day. Felt whacked.
20th May	I read-in the part of Mary as my Principal was absent. Firth Shepherd was there.
21st May	Everyone was worried about the possibility of invasion.
27th May	Met Smith and Ralph for lunch at Scott's. Good journey up to Blackpool. Digs on Park Road a bit squalid. Went for a walk with Margaret Scudamore, Mrs Ebley in the play. She was Michael Redgrave's mother.
28th May	Out in the sunshine. Sat on the pier in the morning. Dress rehearsal from 8a.m. to 1pm. Jack Buchanan very good as Lord Dilling.
29th May	Sat on pier again. Opening night of the show which went well. Afterwards, drink with Austin and Bryan.
1st June	Understudy rehearsal.
2nd June	Went for a walk by the sea. Wild white horses. Watched the show.
3rd June	Understudy rehearsal. Firth was there and was pleased. Watched the evening show. I was so lonely.
4th June	Sunday. Moved to new digs. Lovely coal fire.
6th June	Invasion. Walked by the sea alone.

8th June	Saw 'The Nelson Touch' with Tony Shaw who was playing the Hon. Willy Wynton. Tried on Ann's costume. Had chat with Jack Buchanan and drinks with Austin, Bryan and Frances Rowe.
10th June	Chatted with Ann, my Principal. Watched show with Firth and Winifred (who understudied Margaret Scudamore) in a box. Had drink with Ann.
11th June	Sunday. Up at six. (Ugh!) And fairly good journey back to town with Athene and Margaret.
12th June	Two alerts. Didn't sleep till four am.
13th June	Rehearsal - Tony Guthrie there. Saw Job's 'Uncle Harry' starring Michael Redgrave at the Garrick Theatre.
14th June	Walked in Regent's Park. Rehearsal at 5:00p.m. Ann late for evening performance but not off.
15th June	First night of Cheyney. A glamorous occasion and a warm reception.
16th June	Frances, my Principal was so late that I got made up but she arrived just in time to go on.
17th June	Walked in from Baker Street. Matinee. There were six alerts. Tea in Coal Hole, the basement pub next to the theatre.
18th June	Cheyney notices were very good indeed. The dramatic critic George Bishop said "Firth Shepherd has put this Tyrone Guthrie production on sumptuously." The ladies costumes were designed by Sophie Harris (Motleys) and were in period down to the underwear. The set was painted by the

well-known scenic artists, the Harkers. He was also praised for casting it superbly. Firth Shepherd once said that it was the one among all his productions of which he was most proud. Coral got specially good reviews. Bishop describing the performance as a "fine studied piece of comedy with as much emotion behind it as the author allows." Philip Page, dramatic critic of the Daily Mail's weekly feature wrote, "I venture to award several prizes. Among them to Miss. Coral Brown in the Last of Mrs. Cheyney" and he later praised her again "Coral Brown's performance in the Last of Mrs. Cheyney and Ralph Lynn's in 'Is You Honeymoon Really Necessary?' are among the best individual performances currently appearing in the West End." He headed the list with tributes to Laurence Olivier as Richard the Third and Gielgud as Hamlet. "Distinguished company indeed".

19th June   Walked in the park. When I got back to my flat I saw that the door had been smashed in. The damage had been caused by a pilot-less plane. Went out to Staines with Dick. A dreadful night, nine bombs fell fairly near. We sat on a sofa in the basement of the hotel and he told me how much he loved me.

20th June   Up from Staines. Saw the film 'The Way Ahead'.

21st June   Understudy rehearsal and two shows. Out with Evelyn and Ross. "She's going to have a baby... lucky devil."

22nd June	Raids continued. To Lords. Keith Miller made fifty. Had strawberries and cream. Felt very tired but it was a wonderful day.
23rd June	Last night was noisy. Collected for Red Cross at the theatre. Understudy rehearsal.
24th June	After evening show. Caught the eight-forty to Staines. Went for walk with Dick. We spent the night in hotel basement. Couldn't sleep.
25th June	Rowed boat with Dick on the river.
26th June	Back to town. Hair appointment. Very noisy night. Show had gone well. Spent night in basement in flat.
27th June	Lunch at Kettners. Raids and a stormy day.
28th June	More raids. Understudy rehearsal and two shows.
29th June	Walked in Regent's Park.
30th June	In the morning Regent's Street was bombed. I was in a bus and saw the shop windows shattered all down the right hand side of the street. Had lunch with Jack at Marsham Court. In the afternoon I sat in a deck chair in St. James's Park and wept - I think the cause was mainly exhaustion. And I had the spooky feeling that the bombs were following me about.
1st July	Two shows. Then drinks with Austin and Bryan. Bombs were falling.
2nd July	It had been a bad night of bombing. Sat in Regent's Park.
3rd July	Saw film 'Aux Bas Fonds' with Frank Ross.
6th July	Boiling hot day. Sat in park again.
7th July	Heard that Smith had been given an offer to bring Honeymoon in to the Duke of Yorks.

11th July	In to Smith's office where I met Winifred Shotter.
12th July	Heard that Vernon Kelso wouldn't come into town with Honeymoon. "Was he afraid to be in London?"
17th July	Supper with Hubert at the Savoy.
19th July	I was told that Honeymoon was coming in but that Firth Shepherd wouldn't release me to play the lady's maid Marie. At first I was upset but later thought that this might be a blessing in disguise.
20th July	Saturday. Saw two shows afterwards. Had drinks with Bryan and actor Billy Milton.
29th July	Raids all day.
31st July	Saw 'Honeymoon' dress rehearsal.
1st August	Saw film 'Pin-Up Girl'. First night of 'Honeymoon' a great success.
3rd August	Went with Vernon, Hazel and Saxon Snell the agent to a party at the Savoy.
4th August	Party at St. Mary's Hospital. Dick tried to make ardent love to me - "rather annoyed me".
5th August	Saturday. Tea with Winifred. Then we sat in the Temple Gardens between shows.
6th August	Grand notices for 'Honeymoon'. "Farce has never been more brilliantly handled than in 'Is Your Honeymoon Really Necessary' at the Duke of Yorks." (This was from Philip Page, the dramatic critic).
9th August	A good understudy rehearsal. Sat in the Temple Gardens again.
10th August	A rocket attack.

11th August	At Lord's all day. Had drinks with Percy Chapman in his box.
12th August	Dick took my luggage to the new flat I had just taken in Palmer Street, Victoria. It was just round the corner from Caxton Hall.
13th August	Sunday. Busy all day. Unpacked. "Heaven!".
15th August	Another busy day cleaning the flat.
16th August	A number of raids. Rehearsal was chaotic.
17th August	Housework in the morning. Saw 'Tomorrow The World', featuring a brilliant child actor, David O'Brien.
18th August	Saw a good film, 'The White Cliffs of Dover'.
19th August	Cleaned flat. Felt worried about my family in Derby because of the continuous raids over the Midlands.
26th August	Two shows. Tea with Margaret Scudamore, Madge and Winifred. Dick came to evening performance. Walked back to the flat with him along the embankment. The river was like a Whistler painting.
28th August	Lunch at Sheekeys.
29th August	Met Roland Culver and his wife at Gow's Restaurant
31st August	Met Stanley French, Firth Shepherd's general manager.
1st September	Did my first stint at the Stage Door Canteen. This was a club in Piccadilly and its function was to provide entertainment for the troops on leave in London. I had been interviewed by Catherine Nesbitt for the job. Actresses who

volunteered to work there always had a stringent interview to make sure that only bona fide ones were employed and not girls, or possibly tarts, merely wanting to meet celebrities.

2nd September   Winifred came to tea. She loved the flat. So did I.

4th September   At Stage Door Canteen. Beatrice Lillie did her turn.

5th September   Lunch at the Ritz.

7th September   Hubert and David came to tea at flat.

8th September   Lunch at Gows. Walked across St. James's Park back to flat.

9th September   Over to the Cables with Dick for lunch and dashed back for show.

11th September   Stage Door Canteen again. Helped to serve drinks with stage and film star Elizabeth Allan.

12th September   Awful night with air-raids. Didn't sleep much.

15th September   Vernon, Hazel and Ming for tea.

16th September   My birthday (Twenty-eight). Two shows. Heard that Tehran won the St. Leger. To Savoy for lunch with Dick, Ian and two girls.

19th September   Lunch with Smith and dumb blonde - a waste of oysters! Saw excellent film 'Double Indemnity' starring Barbara Stanwyck. To Stage Door Canteen, Jennifer Gray there.

21st September   Saw Richard III at the New Theatre. Ralph Richardson played Richmond superbly. Reading that entry I found it strange that

	I had not made a mention of Olivier in his outstanding performance as Richard.
23rd September	Jasmine and I met for tea at the Aldwych Corner House.
24th September	Air-raid. Supper with Evelyn and Ross.
25th September	Lunch at Scotts. To Stage Door Canteen for a meeting.
29th September	Met Harold French, actor and producer.
30th September	Two shows. Tea with Austin, Winifred, Madge and Bryan.
3rd October	A good evening at the Stage Door Canteen. Gertrude Lawrence there.
10th October	Lunch with Smith and Ralph at Scotts. Oysters.
11th October	Met Ben Traver's son, Benjy. To Palladium to see Tommy Trinder with a strong company including Elizabeth Welsh, Zoë Gail and the Dagenham Girl Pipers.
13th October	Lunch at the Lantern. Saw 'The Hairy Ape' with Bryan.
16th October	To Hungaria. Tom Webster and Tommy Trinder were there.
17th October	Stage Door Canteen.
18th October	Supper with Saxon Snell and Smith at La Coquille.
19th October	Lunch at Ritz. Saw Somerset Maugham's 'The Circle' at the Haymarket. Yvonne Arnaud exquisite in the scene with Leslie Banks.
21st October	Met Dick and Lance Bromley (who later had a distinguished career at St. Mary's Hospital).

	To Cables pub. They both stayed overnight in the flat.
27th October	Met Ben Travers and Ralph for lunch at La Coquille.
29th October	Entertained Sparkie and Saxon Snell to tea at flat.
30th October	Winifred went on for Margaret Scudamore.
31st October	Stage Door Canteen.
3rd November	Went to Equity meeting. Roger Livesey spoke well. Met Malcolm Sergeant who was AGAIN rather flirtatious!
12th November	A rocket fell very near my flat.
13th November	Hair appointment. Saw John Van Druten's 'Old Acquaintance' at the Apollo starring Edith Evans.
17th November	To dance with Dick and my twin Joan. We met the famous consultant Dickson Wright as we were leaving. Joan and Dick slept at flat.
18th November	Joan came to 'Cheyney' matinee.
19th November	To Palace Theatre for the Green Room Rag, compered by Naunton Wayne. An excellent show which included Margot Fonteyn and Robert Helpmann from Sadlers Wells Ballet in 'Façade' and Moira Shearer in 'Polka'. Then there were George Lacy, the famous pantomime Mother Goose. Zoe Gail and the Dagenham Girl Pipers.
22nd November	Saw Dan O'Neill in Firth Shepherd's office.
23rd November	Saw Gielgud's Hamlet at the Haymarket. (The second time I'd seen it). My only diary entry was "Oh god!".

27th November	Hair appointment. Met Jack for lunch at the Mayfair club. Rather fun.
28th November	Had photos taken by Alexander Bender.
29th November	Stage Door Canteen
30th November	Saw film 'Laura' with Vernon, Hazel and Ralph.
5th December	Lunch at the Woodstock Pub, just off Oxford Street. Then we saw Sid Field in 'Strike It Again' at the Prince of Wales Theatre. He was wonderful, especially in his golfing sketch. To Stage Door Canteen.
12th December	A. V. Alexander the First Lord of the Admiralty was there.
13th December	Rehearsal. Lunch with Liz Duncan and Fay. Supper with Ben and Ralph.
14th December	Saw film about Chopin.
15th December	Supper with Ben Travers, Kenneth Cove and Ralph.
17th December	Down to Staines. A good concert with Dorothy Carless. I met Stinker Murdoch and Tommy Handley's 'Mrs. Mop'.
18th December	Saw Joseph Kesselrig's 'Arsenic and Old Lace' starring Lillian Braithwaite at the Palace Theatre.
21st December	Saw J. M. Barrie's Peter Pan. Frances Day was not right for Peter; the reaction of the children to "Do you believe in fairies?" was delightfully responsive.
22nd December	I went on for Ann Firth at the evening performance. Ann and Frances had often arrived late at the theatre after "the half" (in fact thirty-

five minutes was called before curtain up.) This rule was not always taken very seriously by two of my Principals. When they arrived late I had to be ready, made-up and in costume. On this occasion Ann was later than ever. Athene Seyler, who knew how she had been treating me, took it on herself to tell me to go on. In the one scene I had with Jack Buchanan he "gave me the stage". That is, he let me play upstage of him. Truly the action of a gentleman. I had always found Athene very supportive and I remember that she once asked me into her dressing room and proceeded to give me a short but valuable lesson on the technique of how to use the angles of the head. She took my chin in her hand and moved my head in different directions, asking me to look at myself in the mirror to see the effect. And she said something which I've never forgotten, either when acting or directing, which was that standing three quarters of the way on to an audience has more impact than standing in profile to them.

23rd December	Jack told me that I had been first class.

23rd December — Jack told me that I had been first class.

24th December — Went back to Derby.

25th December — Christmas Day. Quite enjoyable.

26th December — Up at six a.m. Back to town, to Stage Door Canteen. The Free French were there.

28th December — Saw James Bridie's play 'It Depends What You Mean' starring Alastair Sim at the Westminster Theatre.

29th December — Fog. Awful day. I looked for new digs. I could no longer afford to pay for my Palmer Street flat. (£4.00 per week and salary £6.00).

31st December   Went to see American Football at the White City. Before continuing my 1945 diary here are some examples of the advice, given in programmes on what to do if there was an air-raid warning while a performance was in progress. This gives some idea of the atmosphere.

"In the event of an air-raid warning an announcement will be made by means of an illuminated box sign installed in front of the footlights. Patrons are advised to remain in the theatre, but those wishing to leave will be directed to the nearest official shelter after which the performance will continue as long as is practicable."

When I read this I took it to mean "as long as the theatre hasn't had a direct hit and is still standing".

And "If a public air-raid warning is sounded in the course of a performance, the audience will be notified by an illuminated sign in front of the footlights. This does not necessarily mean that an air-raid will take place, and we recommend you to remain in the theatre. If, however you wish to leave, you are at liberty to do so. All we ask, if you feel you must go is that you will depart quietly and, as far as possible, without disturbing others."

And "the RAIDERS PAST signal will also be shown on the illuminated box". Another instruction that was frequently given was "All we ask is that if you feel you must go that you will depart quietly and without excitement." An example, surely, of the British stiff-upper-lip.

The spirit of defiance typical of London at this time was illustrated by the usual brief announcement "All those desiring to leave the theatre may do so but the performance will continue." During the eight months' run of 'Mrs. Cheyney' very few members of the audience took advantage of this offer during air-raid warnings. I thought the majority were more concerned about appearing cowardly than about the possibility of being bombed.

So ended 1944. With daytime air-raids, pilot-less bombs and rockets, with sleepless nights spent in shelters, basements and cellars and with strict food rationing. It also marked the end of my touring days and my arrival in the West End and now I looked forward to a bright future if I managed to survive.

Rona Laurie with Ralph Lynn in 'Outrageous Fortune' at the 'Winter Garden Theatre' (now the New London - Drury Lane).

ℰᴐXVIIɢ
1945

THE ASSASSIN. V.E. Day

1ˢᵗ January	Had an awful day looking for digs.
2ⁿᵈ January	Managed to fix some and was greatly relieved.
3ʳᵈ January	Understudy rehearsal. I gave a farewell party to mark my leaving the Palmer Street flat.
4ᵗʰ January	Dan O'Neill, Firth Shepherd's production manager phoned me and offered me a part in their new production 'The Assassin' by Irwin Shaw which was to follow 'Mrs. Cheyney' at the Savoy. The play was a reconstruction of the intrigues leading to the assassination of Darlan, a French admiral, by the underground movement of the Free-French in Algiers. He was thinly disguised in the play in the character of Admiral Vespery. My part was one of the Free-French fighters.

This was my second engagement with the Shepherd management. Later he was to cast me in his production of 'Stage Door'. I believe now that this was the result of Coral's influence. But I always got on equally well with both of them. He died at the age of fifty-seven, and I went with Bryan to his funeral service at St. Martin in the Fields. The congregation was packed with actors and actresses who had worked for him over the years. While Dvorak's New World Symphony was being played I looked round and saw that Coral, who had been his mistress, was in tears, as were nearly everyone else. He was truly a man of the theatre and I feel privileged to have worked for him.

Left Palmer street. Saw 'Goody Two Shoes' at the Coliseum. Cast included Naughton and Gold, Pat Kirkwood, Fred Emney and the Tiller Girls.

5th January	Out to Staines for New Year party and dance.
9th January	Stage Door Canteen
10th January	Found a flat in Bryanston Street, St. Marylebone - not so bad so I took it for six months.

I have lived in St. Marylebone ever since, moving to New Quebec Street, just around the corner. My flat is opposite a famous pub, 'The Bricklayers' Arms'. When Elizabeth Taylor and Richard Burton came to London she asked to be taken to a typical English pub. I was having a drink there that evening and saw them standing at the bar. The regulars were taking no notice of them and there was an amusing photograph in the paper the next day.

26th January	Lunch at La Coquille with Vernon, Hazel, Guy Fane and Ralph. Then we saw Philip King's farce 'See How They Run' at the Comedy Theatre. "Terrible except for Johnny Deverell".

Tea with Pat Hicks (ex RADA) and Saxon Snell. Saw Evelyn's baby, Neilson, (he is now making a successful career in America as a presenter on television).

27th January	The blind "VC" came to the Savoy for the matinee. I sat next to him in the stalls and described the action to him. Later it turned out that he was an impostor, not blind at all, and didn't have an artificial leg. Someone saw him in a corridor at the Savoy hotel and whacked him on the shins with a stick. He had already taken in several West End Stars including Jack, Coral and Ralph - and me.

28th January	Saw film 'Mrs. Parkington'
30th January	Saw 'Babes in the Wood' at His Majesties. Leo Franklyn was Dame Trot and Monsewer Eddie Gray, Baron Stoney. Stage Door Canteen. Heard that the 'blind VC' had been rumbled. Jack and Coral laughed.
31st February	Air-raid
1st February	Saw 'Three's A Family' at the Saville Theatre
2nd February	To Jacqumar for costume fitting. To Stage Golfing Society in the evening.
3rd February	Moved into new flat in Bryanston Street. Dinner with Jack Thomas, house manager at the Savoy Theatre.
4th February	Saw 'Guest In the House'. The show was given for charity.
5th February	Matinee Cheyney. Went to Stage Golfing Society.
6th February	Saw film 'Woman in the Window'. Stage Door Canteen.
7th February	To Savoy to say goodbye to the company. It had been a most happy engagement.
11th February	Home to Derby.
12th February	Lunch at the Friary Hotel with Harriette Johns, who was on a prior-to-London tour of Vernon Sylvaine's 'Madame' starring Robertson Hare and Alfred Drayton.
13th February	Back to London. To Stage Golfing Society in the evening.
14th February	To Jacqumar and Jaeger for costume fittings. To Stage Golfing Society in the evening.

15th February	Lunch with Barry O'Brien at the Moulin D'Or. Saw film 'Together Again'. Irene Dunne was very good. To Stage Golfing Society again. Met the actor Harold Warrender.

Into the Savoy for a first reading of 'The Assassin'. The action moved from the meeting place of the Underground movement in Algiers, to the Admiral's headquarters and finally to the death cell. It had an enormous cast, headed by Barry Morse and Rosalyn Boulter. And there was a strong supporting company.

20th February	Started rehearsing. Marcel Varnel had already directed several plays for Firth including 'The Man Who Came To Dinner', 'Arsenic and Old Lace', 'Junior Miss', 'My Sister Eileen', 'Halfway To Heaven' and 'Tomorrow The World'. He was very technical and demanding and I felt deadbeat after this first rehearsal.
22nd February	Felt that my part was coming out well and that I was going to like it.
25th February	To christening party for Evelyn's son, Neilson Ross. Champagne.
26th February	Rehearsal. To Jacqumar for a fitting.
4th March	We rehearsed in the room in Soho the scene of Mrs. Cheyney rehearsals.
5th March	Rehearsal on the set for the first time. Scenery had been painted by the Harkers and was exquisite.
6th March	Busy day rehearsing, trying on costumes and make-up.
7th March	Dress-rehearsal - great fun and my clothes were approved. But I thought that the play only had a fifty-fifty chance at success.

9th March	Hazel and Vernon were married.
10th March	Company travelled to Bournemouth in a Ladies Only Carriage. I had booked in at the Westover Hotel - very comfortable.
12th March	Show opened - a great success.
13th March	Pat and I walked by the sea.
14th March	Morning rehearsal. Martin Walker couldn't stay the course and left the cast - a pity. He was one of the most relaxed actors that I have ever seen.
15th March	Rehearsal for the new people. We were being worked very hard.
16th March	Morning rehearsal. I was glad that the hotel was so comfortable.
17th March	Two shows. Had drinks with Arthur Young who was playing Vespery.
18th March	Back to town. Actor Terence de Marney was in our carriage. Back to flat to discover that a rocket had fallen at Marble Arch and had blown out two of my big front windows. Felt tired, depressed and alone.
19th March	Rehearsed at Aldwych.
20th March	First dress-rehearsal went very smoothly and now I was happy about the show.
21st March	Public dress-rehearsal. A great thrill and the audience loved it. To Stage Golfing Society.
22nd March	Opening night at the Savoy Theatre. I was very calm. Found thirty telegrams at the theatre and flowers. Went to party that Philip Page was giving at the Dorchester.

23rd March	A grand press. "I have just looked up my old reviews." "There are acceptable performances by Miss Rona Laurie, Mr Charles Rolf, Mr Charles Quatermaine, and Mr. John. E. Coyle (The Times) and the women characters will be almost negligible were they not played with such attractive charm by Miss Rosalyn Boulter and Miss Rona Laurie: and for bonnie Rona Laurie I do not doubt that many men would lay them doon and dee" (Philip Page - The Daily Mail).
24th March	It was all a great thrill and the diary note was "I think I am on the right track at last!". Stage Golfing Society. Out to two shows.
27th March	A photo call with Alexander Bender. He fell off the front of the Savoy Stage as he was backing to get a wider picture and landed in the orchestra pit with his camera on top of him, but luckily he was only bruised.
29th March	Another photo call but we were free by lunchtime.
30th March	Good Friday. No show.

No entries in the diary until 23rd April. My social life was obviously not so strenuous just then.

23rd April	Took Teresa (Toppet) and Toby Robertson out to tea.
25th April	Ben and his daughter José came to the show and I had supper with them afterwards. We were joined by Bunny Hare and his friend the actress Constance Lorne.
26th April	Lunch at La Coquille. After the show I went to Dorothy Ward's birthday party in her flat in Chiltern Court, St. Marylebone. A galaxy of stars were there. When I was introduced to

James Agate, the dramatic critic of the Sunday Times, he remained seated and just grunted.

27th April	Down to Cookham with Barry O'Brien for lunch. My new white dress was a great success at the St. Mary's dance that night.
29th April	Sunday. Went down to Esher with Jack. Lunch at the Bear. Tea at Danito's and dinner at the Berkeley buttery.
1st May	Had a sitting for my portrait. Saw the film 'Going My Way' - Excellent.
2nd May	Saw Eden Philpotts' 'Yellow Sands' at the Westminster and chatted afterwards with Cedric Hardwicke. Went to party at the Comedy Theatre. George Gee - welcoming.
4th May	Had long sitting for my portrait. Saw the film 'The Picture of Dorian Gray'. "Excellent - specially the scene in the night-club with Angela Lansbury singing about "the little yellow bird".
5th May	After show went to the Cabaret club and on to the Astor. "Loathed it".
6th May	Walked round Hyde Park. Felt nervy.
7th May	Drink with Saxon Snell at Stage Golfing Society.
8th May	V.E. Day. Drinks with Dick at the Cables then lunch at La Coquille, afterwards to Victoria Palace. At this point in my diary the entries stopped and with the end of the war in Europe a chapter of my life and five years of wartime conditions and bombing were over. I have never since experienced a period of such intense existence with its mixture of tragedy and joy, of success and failure set against the background of war.

❧ EPILOGUE ❧

Now I am in my nineties and still coaching students, my love of the theatre undiminished. When a new one arrives in my flat to be prepared for an audition to a drama school the adrenaline starts to flow and I feel as if I have had a blood transfusion. It is particularly rewarding to work on the speech which they have chosen from Shakespeare. Today's youngsters usually find modern playwrights far easier to tackle than the classics. Time has become more and more precious to me. When I was told about the art critic Bernard Berenson, who loved life so much that when he was ninety said, "I would willingly stand at street corners, hat in hand, asking passers-by to drop their unused minutes in it" I could identify with him and with another attitude to old age written by W. B. Yates.

> 'An aged man is but a paltry thing,
> A tattered coat upon a stick, unless
> Soul clap it's hands and sing and louder sing
> For every tatter in it's mortal dress'

Yes indeed.

Although I still have a lively interest in the theatre today, read reviews and go to plays, I avoid the revivals of those classics which I saw when they were originally produced. Too often now they are up-dated to make them 'relevant' to today's audiences and used to demonstrate the Director's originality. Charles Lamb wrote "Amid the mortifying circumstances attendant on growing old, it is something to have seen 'The School for Scandal' in its glory".

And I am lucky enough to be of an age to have seen the outstanding actors of the twentieth century. There are four performances which have made an indelible impression on me; John Gielgud's Hamlet, Ralph Richardson's Falstaff, Donald Wolfit's King Lear and Laurence Olivier's Archie Rice in John Osborne's 'The Entertainer'. I continue to enjoy teaching. The poet Philip

Larkin wrote about work, which he compared to a toad, and the comfort it can bring in later life.

'Give me your arm, old toad,
Help me down Cemetery Road'

And certainly I find that work has been a great support to me down that Cemetery Road on which we are all travelling. And one is always learning. As Geoffrey Chaucer said four hundred years ago

'The lyf so short, the craft so long to lerne'

Rona Laurie

St. Marylebone

Printed in Great Britain by
Amazon.co.uk, Ltd.,
Marston Gate.